Grand Solar Minimum: Ice Age

Introduction

With so much discussion about global warming it is often forgotten that we are still living in the Quarternary Ice Age!

In 2009 I submitted an idea for a thesis about a coming ice age and the prospect of looming energy insecurity. However my idea for a Phd was not accepted as the supervisor thought it was too far- fetched!

So I wrote several articles instead about cold weather and a looming energy gap that were published in newspapers such as the Oxford times. Now suddenly

It seems that the idea of a mini ice is becoming a serious topic for discussion.

Even Jon Gribbin who wrote the seminal book called Hothouse Earth about global warming has now changed his mind and written a short new book on the ice age theory !

Recently a NASA satellite in Antarctica recorded the coldest temperature on our planet, an astonishing low of minus 94.7 C. There has been so much publicity about anthropogenic global warming that many readers will be surprised to learn that we are technically still living in an ice age at the present time! This present ongoing great ice age is called the Quarternary ice age.

   This ice age started 2.58 million years ago. Surprisingly this Quarternary ice age is the coldest period on Earth for the last 500 million years! These long time scales help imbue a sense of perspective that is often lacking when discussions of Earth`s climate take place. The entire Quaternary Period is referred to as an ice age because at least one permanent large ice sheet, such as the Antarctic ice sheet, has existed continuously during this time.

   The Arctic ice became a fixture later, at around two and a half million years ago. For the last two and half million years there has been ice at both poles and plentiful snow accumulations elsewhere.

Throughout the Quarternary era, large ice sheets and glaciers have continually advanced and retreated. It is perfectly normal for glaciers to grow and melt during the ice ages. We see the same thing happening today. It is also perfectly normal for large chunks of ice to break off and fall into the sea.

A large rift has recently appeared on the Larsen C ice shelf in Antarctica. This process is called calving and occurs when the ice becomes eroded by the sea. This entirely natural phenomenon has been seized upon as evidence of a global warming, but in fact calving has occurred throughout the ice ages.

In 2017 a large chunk of the Antarctic ice shelf calved and floated away. This did not cause a rise in the sea level however, since the ice is already floating on the water. According to NASA Goddard Institute for Space Studies the Larsen ice calving event contributed to a mere 0.1 mm rise in sea level! When you float ice cubes in a drink and the ice melts, your drink does not overflow!

Since the Antarctic ice shelves are floating in water they will not raise sea levels if they melt. The calving process is a normal sign of a healthy ice sheet that periodically sheds its load in order to maintain homeostasis. This is because frequent heavy snow falls will cause the ice sheet to become heavy and unbalanced and therefore a calving has to take place.

Although we are in the midst of the Quaternary Ice Age, we are fortunate to be living in one of the interglacials of this formidable ice age. The interglacials of the Quaternary ice age generally have a length of between 10-12,000 years. Ice ages have shaped human civilisation. The gift of fertile soil to farmers is the legacy of the last ice age.

The breadbaskets in America, and the nutrient rich soil of Great Britain, were enhanced when the ice retreated. Human civilisation has been flourishing for nearly twelve thousand years in a balmy interglacial.

What does this mean exactly? It means that we could be at the very end of our warm weather interglacial. We are now hurtling towards a major glaciation event and a recurrence of the great ice age!

The present geologic eon is the Phanerozoic Eon, which spans the past 545 million years. This Eon encompasses twelve periods. These lengthy periods spanning millions of years each are known as; the Cambrian, the Ordovician, the Silurian, the Devonian, the Carboniferous, the Permian, the Triassic, Jurassic, the Cretaceous, Paleogne (emcompassing the Paleocene, the Eocene and the Oligocene) the Neogene, and finally the Quarternary Period.

Readers may be familiar with the Triassic, Jurassic period as being the time of the dinosaurs. The fertile Carboniferous period had warm tropical swamps and huge trees that created many of the carbon coal deposits buried deep underground that are mined today.

During our Phanerozoic Eon, planet Earth has endured several frozen climate cycles, some lasting 50 to 90 million years. The present day Quarternary ice age period is the shortest geologic period in the Phanerozoic Eon.

The Quartenary divides into the frozen Pleistocene ice age, and the present day Holocene interglacial which has seen mankind flourish with its favourable weather conditions.

This benevolent interlude of interglacial warmth may be about to change as the Holocene is due to end with the dawn of a new ice age. Why did the climate become so much colder during the last 2.5 million years?

One of the reasons for this colder climate is that warm ocean currents became blocked when South America moved towards joined North America. The Panamanian Isthmus then became a land bridge. This bridge then disrupted and blocked the warm Pacific Ocean waters, thereby preventing them from mixing with the much colder Atlantic Ocean waters.

This Panamanian Isthmus then gave rise to the thermohaline circulation that is part of the Gulf Stream. Because of this geological formation of the land bridge, ice was able to accumulate at the Arctic and has remained there ever since. This example shows how a tectonic structural change in land mass can affect the climate (Oceanus 2017).

The Antarctic had already been ice capped for millions of years after Gondwanaland broke up. Gondwana was originally part of the supercontinent Pangaea. The land mass started to separate during the Jurassic period. When this super continent divided the Antarctic region was left isolated from warmer ocean currents and became frozen. The Arctic North

Pole then also froze up after the Panamanian land bridge was formed.

The opening and closing of seaways has a profound effect on the heat that is transported by ocean waters. A slight tilt of the Earth on its axis 2.5 million years ago might have resulted in less sunlight in the Northern Hemisphere. So now both Poles had permanent ice caps that have lasted to the present day. Despite fears that they will melt, this is highly unlikely due to the aforementioned factors.

The ice ages that form part of the present ongoing ice age, the Quarternary, usually last for around 90-100, 000 years. This figure is based on the research of husband and wife team

John and Katherine Imbrie who have written many books on the history of Earth's great ice ages. At the grand finale of an ice age there is a rapid transition to an interglacial. Indeed prehistoric man living in the freezing ice age conditions could have literally woken up one day to find that the ice was melted.

Within a decade or so our surprised ancestors could have unexpectedly found themselves living in a balmy paradise! So it seems that a transition from an ice age to an interglacial can happen very rapidly. Therefore one could surmise that the converse could occur, and that an ice age may arrive just as rapidly within a few decades. Indeed the geologic temperature graphs show a rapid descent into an ice age has taken place previously.

The Earth has always existed in one of three conditions. These three conditions are a greenhouse, an icehouse and a snowball Earth. The last two million years have been mostly very cold on our planet with ice caps covering much of Europe, Asia, North America and two thirds of the British Isles.

The "Icehouses" are about 5°C colder than the four warmer epochs known as "Greenhouses". Millions of years ago dinosaurs basked in tropical sunshine in England.

Alligators roamed as far north as present day Alaska! There was no ice present at either of the Poles or indeed anywhere on the Earth. The Earth was then in a *real green house* state. A proper greenhouse in scientific terms is when there is not a trace of snow or ice on planet Earth. Our planet has since passed into an *ice house* state. The present ice house state is the reason that we presently have plentiful snow and ice at both North and South Poles. We are already living in an ice house condition and soon it will get much colder.

Earth has also been in a snowball condition where the entire globe was covered in snow and ice. "Snowball" Earth condition is thankfully very rare. The last snowball Earth event is known as the Cryogenian.

The snowball began 850 million years ago and globally temperatures were minus 12 degrees below freezing. Land froze over and seas turned to slushy ice. Snowball Earth is very rare thankfully, as were it to occur today, life on Earth would all but be wiped out. It is an amazing concept that the Equator was once covered in ice!

A 2010 study by Harvard scientists shows that the Earth did indeed freeze over like a snowball (MacDonald 2010). Imagine a scenario where the tropical equatorial zones are frozen and the oceans are nearly frozen. The evidence from geologic sediments does indeed point to the Equator once having Arctic conditions. Resilient life forms persisted in the cold oceans. The snowball finally melted 636 million years ago. When the snowball finally thawed life exploded across the planet in an evolutionary burst.

There are many theories as to how this snowball event happened. One of these theories points out that the sun was much weaker at that time. The sun has been shown to regularly fluctuate in output and this variability and its effect on climate will be discussed in this book.

The Sun may also have influenced the melting of the snowball as the Earth`s orbital tilt changed so allowing more warmth from the sun`s rays to penetrate the ice. Underwater volcanic eruptions may have helped trigger the great melting of the giant snowball.

At the present time we are actually living in an icehouse condition. This fact may seem at odds with all of the media attention that is focussing on a runaway global warming greenhouse scenario for our precious planet. Currently global temperatures are just 5 degrees Celsius above the previous global temperatures during the last ice age. Therefore we are not so far off an ice age already.

During the past two million year ice age freeze of the Northern Hemisphere, the climate has been glacial for 90 per cent of the time. This ice age freeze has been punctuated by short warm periods totalling a mere ten per cent of the overall time period.

Therefore ninety per cent of the last two million years on planet Earth has been extremely cold and very thick ice sheets have amassed. The remaining ten per cent of the warmer climatic periods is therefore atypical of the climatic norm for our planet.

We are presently living in one of these atypical warmer periods. Worryingly this warm interglacial that we enjoy living in is predicted to end soon if the past data is correct. Those who hope that carbon dioxide levels have risen sufficiently to stave off another ice age may be proved wrong. Northern Hemisphere winters have recently accumulated similar snow cover to that of the previous ice ages.

This extensive snow cover is clearly shown from photographs taken from the air during recent snowy winters. The warning signs are all pointing to the onset of the expected ice age and we will be powerless to prevent it!

The Northern Hemisphere currently experiences heavy snow fall as we are still in the present "icehouse". The reasons for an ice house condition have been speculated to be due to Earth`s passage through a dense matter spiral arm of our Milky Way or it may be a result of structural tectonic break ups on our planet.

Either way the present ice house conditions that we are living in could be about to get a whole lot worse! When our ice age finally arrives with a vengeance we could see a decimation of the population from hypothermia and starvation. The reasons why Earth has been so very cold for the last two million years are not fully known, though there is a theory of that tectonic upheaval and the Panamanian Land Bridge may have triggered the cold Earth condition.

A supercontinent known as Pangea dominated Earth for 160 million years. Pangea later broke apart into the continents of Africa and America. This separation is conjectured to have somehow caused a shift in the climate.

There is scientific evidence that proves that climate was drastically altered as Pangea broke up into large chunks of land masses. When the continents separated a change resulted in the flow of the oceanic currents and winds.

The scientific theory is known as Continental Drift and was created by Alfred Wegener to explain how the continents shifted Earth's surface. This drifting of continents affected aspects such as climate and rock formations. The outcome of Pangea separating was that the world became cooler as the oceans currents became displaced and ice caps were formed.

The Himalayas rose up later in another tectonic upheaval. This mountain formation made the planet cooler by changing wind patterns, according to the Centre for Ice and Climate at the Neils Bohr institute.

Our ever changing planet Earth has experienced five major ice ages that have been named and documented. We are presently in a fifth ice age known as the Quaternary ice age. Prior to the present Quarternary Glaciation there have been four other long lasting ice ages. Before our present ice age there was the Karoo ice age that took place during the Carboniferous and Permian eras 360 to 260 million years ago.

The Karoo ice age was preceded by the Andean –Saharan ice age during the Ordovician and Silurian epochs. This ice age took place 450 to 420 million years ago. The Karoo ice age was preceded by the Cryogenian ice age 850 to 635 million years ago. As its name suggest the Cryogenian ice age was very severely cold. It is theorised that a complete snowball Earth glaciation occurred during the Cryogenian (Kopp et al 2005). It is hypothesised that the snowball finally melted due to a spate of underwater vulcanism that would have warmed the seas. The melting of the giant snowball may have then triggered the so called great oxygenation event that caused an explosion of life on our lifeless frozen planet.

The first recorded ice age is known as the Huronian Ice Age. This took place from 2.4 to 2.1 billion years ago. This ice age led to mass extinction of the primitive bacterial cellular life forms that were emerging. It is thought that the sun shone dimly at that time, making Earth icy cold. Interestingly Kopp`s team discovered that the Earth`s atmosphere became colder when carbon dioxide and water emerged during this time.

This is an unusual finding since both water vapour and carbon dioxide are widely considered to be green house gases! This made the atmosphere thinner and it lost heat. This ice age was triggered by the great oxygenation event that resulted in the formation of carbon dioxide and water which replaced the methane atmosphere. This cooling event is an interesting fact since it is held that carbon dioxide is an important warming greenhouse gas.

Ice core researchers at the Neils Bohr Institute in Denmark discovered that the Earth has been getting gradually cooler over the past 40 to 65 million years. This long term ice core data does help imbue a sense of perspective regarding long term climate change.

We may perceive our climate to be warming in the present day but the fact remains that Earth has been slowly cooling down over the last 40 to 65 million years!

Danish ice core researchers think that this gradual cooling was the result of the continents drifting and altering the temperature somehow by amplifying Earth`s orbital radiation influx. These orbital influences are sometimes covered by the term Milankovitch cycles that are named after the Serbian mathematician Milutin Milankovitch.

The Neils Bohr institute also discovered that during the past 40 million years levels of carbon dioxide have also been falling. Levels of carbon dioxide were once as high as 2000 parts per million (ppm). In contrast today`s levels of carbon dioxide may be rising to a level of 400ppm.

Many concerns have been voiced by this high reading that is blamed on our industrial activities. One can observe that in the long term paleoclimatic history of our planet there have been times when carbon dioxide levels were five times greater than they are in the twenty first century.

Today there is a lot of anxiety about the fact that atmospheric levels of carbon dioxide have been climbing steadily since our industrial revolution in Great Britain. The carbon dioxide levels seem to be slowly creeping up and have now reached the dizzying heights of 400 parts per million.

This relatively modest rise is causing panic among some environmental activists and there have been many protests about climate change. Therefore it is important to take a long term perspective of the Earth and to appreciate that this level of 400 parts per million is well within the range of what is normal for our planet.

   The long term trend is for a cooling Earth. Our planet has steadily cooled over the last 40 million years. This is an important statistic to remember. 40 million years is a long time for a downward trend of global temperature. If the climate became briefly warmer during recent decades this temperature blip would appear as insignificant noise on a long term temperature graph of our planet`s paleoclimate.

   The graph below spans millions of years. There is a linear downward cooling trajectory. We are at the end of the axis in the Pleistocene epoch at the coolest part in Earth`s history.

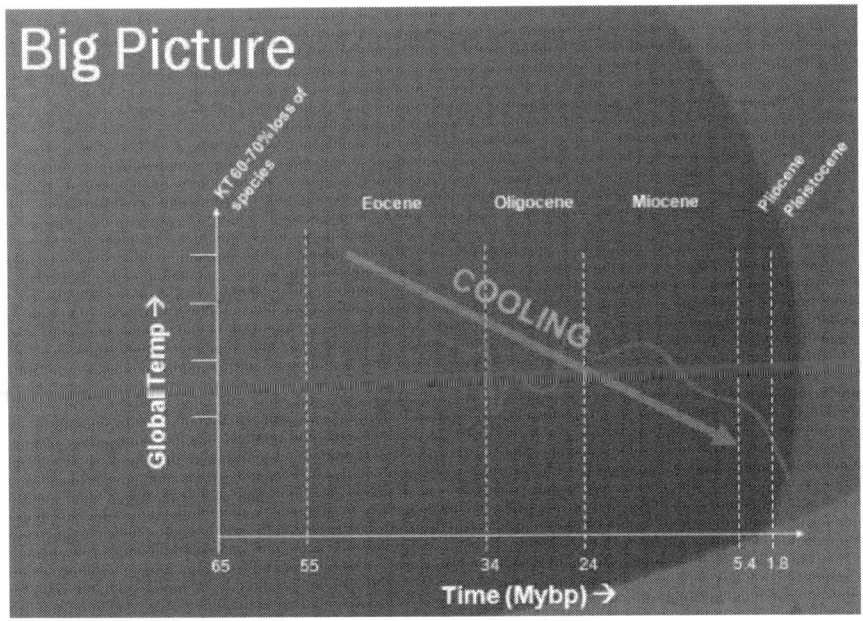

Credit Dandebat/DK

The Pleistocene/ Quarternary epoch started 2.6 million years ago and has consisted of several ice ages. Thus we have an inexorably cooling Earth, though we are presently enjoying an interlude of milder warmer conditions in the Northern Hemisphere. It is important to get the big picture about climate on Earth. The long term trend shows a cooling which may become dangerous to humanity if it continues.

The pattern of ice ages that we presently experience commenced 40 million years ago and seems remarkably durable. It may seem baffling to talk of the prevailing pattern of ice ages when we are enjoying the relatively mild weather of our era.

This is because we are still enjoying our interglacial epoch known as the Holocene. This book will explain why our interglacial may be about to end, and thereby plunging us into an instant ice age of unimaginable severity.

This well known graph of the Pleistocene ice age shows the small areas above the base line which depict the warm interglacials. We presently live in the last circled area above the base line. For the last three million years the majority of the time our planet was in the cold ice ages depicted as shaded areas below the base line.

This graph clearly shows that we are presently in an anomalous period of warmth which may soon be about to end. The precipitous fall into ice age conditions from the peak of an interglacial should give us cause for concern.

The small circles in purple above the axis are in fact our warm interglacials while the large green areas are the ice ages. The diagram of the Pleistocene epoch shows how ice age conditions predominate over the warm interglacials.

The recent long term paleoclimatic trend is for a warm interglacial to last for approximately 11 to 12 thousand years. Mankind has now been enjoying life in the balmy conditions of this interglacial for 11, 726 years to give a more precise measurement.

Therefore we could be about to exit our warm interglacial known as the Holocene. The idea that our greenhouse emissions may stave off this ice age is wishful thinking unfortunately. In past geologic epochs such as the Ordovician, there have been levels of carbon dioxide as high as 3000 ppm and yet the Earth still endured terrible ice ages.

Geological evidence of the last ice age comes from the large displaced rock boulders called erratics. These gigantic boulders have been found all over America. There is even a large erratic boulder in Central Park, New York.

The large boulders were pushed south by the ice sheets. Geologists studying the ice ages have finally explained the mystery of these large boulders called erratics which are found in unusual locations all over America.

The Earth has many strange quirks regarding climate and so we cannot say this departure from the Holocene will definitely occur any day now with total confidence. It is possible that our interglacial might last a lot longer than is the norm.

A longer interglacial has happened in the very distant past. However since the million years long trend shows a cooling of the Earth, this might be overly optimistic. The probabilities are that this ice age coming soon will be the worst ice age on record and may even wipe us out as Earth is inexorably cooling down.

The ice ages used to thaw out every 41 million years. Then this pattern changed to a thawing out once every 100, 000 years. This change to a longer ice age implies an insidious cooling. The Earth is now on an inexorable cooling trend in the paleoclimatic context. Therefore this interglacial may not be late in ending as is optimistically hoped by climate scientists. An ice age could commence during this century or even in a few years time!

There once existed an interglacial that lasted 28 thousand years according to data from the European Project for Ice Coring in Antarctica known by the acronym EPICA. This might give rise to hope that we may now be an interglacial lasting longer than the general duration of around 11, 500years. This is a complex subject and some ice core specialists think that our present glacial may be longer than 11, 700 years. However it would be sensible to prepare ourselves in case the warm Holocene comes to an abrupt end.

When discussing the ice ages it is important to note that the Antarctic and the Arctic behave differently. Whereas the Antarctic has become locked into a more or less fixed cycle of continuous ice, the Northern Hemisphere behaves differently. In the Northern Hemisphere over millions of years, a pattern has developed that differs from that of the South Pole.

The Northern ice sheets and glaciers have developed a pattern of continual advance and retreat which differs from the relatively static pattern of the Southern ice sheets. So the next time you see a time lapse photo of Arctic ice retreating, rest assured that this is how the Arctic ice sheet behaves. The main ice advance cycles have occurred at 21, 41 and 100 ky cycles.

There is often speculation as to how the massive ice sheets in North America could have melted. The thawing of the American Laurentide ice sheet might be explained by the sinking of rock under the colossal weight of the North American ice sheet. After several ice accumulation cycles the Earth's crust sagged so far that the ice's surface was at a low enough altitude to melt in summer.

This is known as isostatic rebound. Geologist Peter Clark of Oregon State University speculates that the melting of ice could have been triggered because the ice sheets had reached such a size that they had become unstable and were ready to go. However isostatic rebound does not explain the exact time scales of the ice ages.

The innovative American geologist, Randall Carlson, thinks that the energy needed to melt the ancient Laurentide ice sheets would be in the region of that produced by thousands of megaton nuclear blasts! So clearly he is not a big fan of the isostatic rebound theory.

Carlson thinks that a super massive event such as a massive solar flare storm or an asteroid impact, maybe even a huge volcanic eruption would be needed to melt this huge ice sheet.

Carlson has a lot of original ideas and he speculates that 11, 600 years ago there was a great flood that destroyed the mythical civilisation of Atlantis that is now below the sea. Atlantis was a

Greek island that Plato wrote of 11, 600 years ago. It is also the time of the ice thaw and melt flood that ended the ice age.

Could the ancient myth of Atlantis possibly be true? Carlson does not subscribe to the popular idea that rising carbon dioxide levels would have been able to melt the very thick frozen ice sheets.

In truth no one really understands how these massive sheets could have melted so suddenly and this is very worrying as there may be cataclysmic events that we are not prepared for. Perhaps the Sun woke up?

The popular theory of the Sun as a variable output star implies that the

Sun could go to sleep during an ice age, in a metaphorical sense. The last ice age may have ended with a frightening bang but we do not know yet how the next ice age will begin. It could begin with a gradual accumulation of snow or with a snowblitz of unprecedented intensity.

The Northern Hemisphere is densely populated as the greater land masses are here. A pattern of heavy snowfall and advancing ice sheets therefore makes the Northern Hemisphere more prone to an ice age. The ice core data implies that the Northern Hemisphere has more to fear from a sudden increase in ice cover as this where the greatest land mass and population lies.

Ice core studies show that prior to the last 40 million years the warm interglacials lasted for much longer time periods. Then something happened to switch this pattern and the warm interglacials began to become shorter. We are presently living in one of these warmer interglacial times of this very severe ice age.

Some scientists think that the Northern Hemisphere may be more vulnerable to small changes in insolation or sunlight reaching the Earth`s surface (Neils Bohr Ice and Climate Unit). This is corroborated by ice core records and the present day phenomenon of Arctic amplification.

Arctic amplification is a process whereby small differences in insolation lead to a disproportionately bigger effect in the poles. The idea that a small change can lead to a larger non linear effect was demonstrated by chaos theory. This concept sometimes known as the butterfly effect will be discussed later in relation to the Earth's climate.

Returning to the present Quarternary ice age, it seems that our present interglacial may soon be ending. The incontrovertible geologic record proves that most interglacials last for around 11, 500 years.

This deduction is based on past geologic records for the Quarternary which is also known as the Pleistocene era. For the past two and a half million years the Quarternary ice age has moved in and out of glacial conditions.

Evidence for past ice ages has come from geological phenomena such as glacial sedimentary till and displaced boulders known as erratics. Geologists found huge boulders which they named erratic. These gigantic rocks had been pushed for miles by moving ice sheets. Ice age landslide debris also scratched the bedrock.

The end of the last ice age may have coincided with a major catastrophe. Earth has suffered at least five major catastrophic extinction events during its turbulent history including the Cretaceous-Tertiary extinction event 65 million years ago that wiped out the dinosaurs. This was preceded by the Permian mass extinction 248 million years ago that wiped out 96% of all species on Earth.

Our catastrophe free interglacial, the Holocene, is unusually calm. While it has been beneficial for humans there is evidence that many species are becoming extinct as a result of unfettered human activity.

This had led scientists to propose that our Holocene be considered as the sixth major extinction event in Earth`s history. The present rate of extinction is around 140, 000 species per year. The Holocene extinction started at the end of the Pleistocene.

At the finale of the last Pleistocene ice age the megafauna or giant animals died out. Gigantic sloths the size of a small truck suddenly died out. Most of the giant sloths, bears, sabre tooth tigers, mammoths and hippos suddenly became extinct 12000 years ago. Perhaps these megafauna were hunted by early humans or perhaps an impact wiped them out. We do not know what caused this Quarternary extinction event that occurred at the end of the last ice age.

It has been speculated that farting mega -herbivores would have contributed to the atmosphere`s greenhouse gas methane! Therefore their extinction and consequent lack of farting warming emissions may have contributed to the subsequent Younger Dryas cooling event! However other studies show a fall rather than a rise in greenhouse gases during the Pleistocene ice age and so this academic area is not settled.

To avoid confusion it should be noted that the terms Pleistocene and Quarternary ice age are both used interchangeably to describe the same ice age. During the Pleistocene-Quarternary ice age epoch the melting events used to take place every 41 thousand years. Then the pattern changed to a melting event every 100, 000 years. So the ice ages now lasted around 90-100, 000 years followed by a melt into an interglacial. This longer

100 000 year thaw cycle is the one we presently live in.

The fact that the pattern shifted to a longer time period has puzzled many glaciologists. It may even indicate that the Earth is gradually getting cooler since the ice ages are now lasting for a much longer duration. What caused the melting events to start taking place at further apart time intervals? This conundrum has been called the 100,000 year problem.

It is also important to make a mental note of this 100, 000 year dilemma because it calls into question the theory of the Milankovitch cycles and orbital timescales which will be discussed later.

The transition from the 41 thousand year intervals to the longer 100, 000 year time interval is known as the Mid Pleistocene Transition or MPT. This transition took place around 800, 000 years ago during the icy Pleistocene epoch.

Why is any of this important I sense my readers are asking? This transition from 41 to 100 thousand years matters because it implies that in the long geologic time frame our planet is getting gradually cooler. Some geophysicists think that the Earth`s core is also getting cooler.

Might there even be a link with a cooling inner core? The Earth`s molten core is 4.6 billion years old and is no longer a teenager. The swirling outer core generates a magnetic field via the rotational coriolis force.

However as will be discussed in the chapter on the magnetic field, there are ominous signs of a magnetic field collapse. A slow cooling trend might explain the Mid Pleistocene Transition. The Earth is no longer thawing out every 41,000 years because it is slowly getting colder.

When the Earth first formed there was plenty of heat in its core and this in turn gave rise to our life giving magnetic field. If the Earth is cooling down this could be a worrying portent. There could even be a cosmic connection causing the insidious cooling such as a dense dusty spiral arm of our Milky Way that is serving to block some of the solar input.

As the diagram below indicates the temperature is gradually falling on planet Earth.

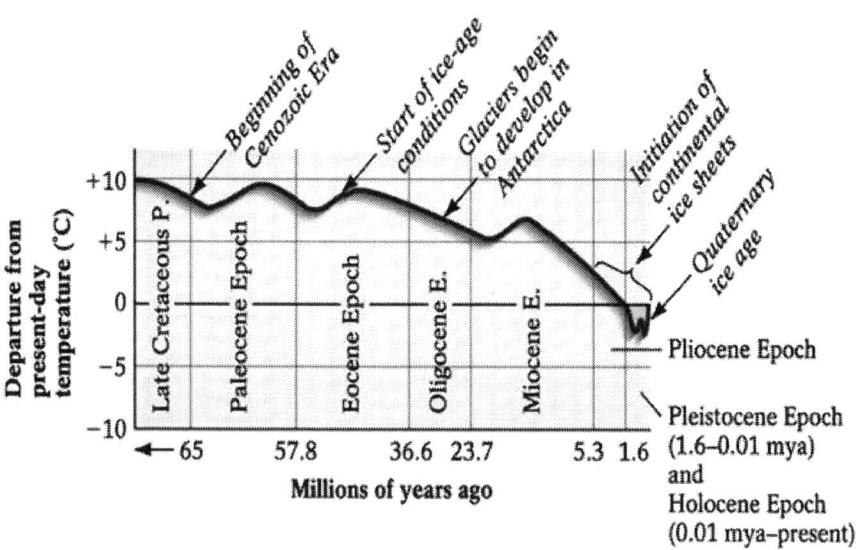

Chapter One: The Sunspot Decline

At the beginning of March 2018 Great Britain experienced very heavy snowfalls due to a change in our usual wind directions. The infamous "Beast from the East" winds from Russia brought record snowfalls in March. This change in wind direction from warm westerly to cold easterly is thought to be affected by the sun.

Professor Mike Lockwood is convinced that a low sunspot count can induce more cold easterly wind flows. **In 2017 Mike Lockwood at the Rutherford Appleton Laboratory in Oxfordshire said that the sunspot activity is** declining at its fastest rate for *ten thousand years*!

Could this be the start of our new ice age? Professor Mike Lockwood of Reading University is concerned about the declining strength of our Sun and its heliosphere. The heliosphere is a protective bubble that deflects nasty space weather away from Earth.

Space weather is loaded with deadly cosmic radiation and energetic gamma rays. Lockwood believes that the heliospheric bubble that is protecting both planet Earth and our solar system will have substantially shrunk by mid century. Then we will be at the mercy of whatever the cosmos decides to throw at us.

The mid century year 2050 is also predicted to be the culmination for three decades of a solar sunspot minimum that may trigger a mini ice age. **Professor Mike Lockwood is a British atmospheric physicist who has carried out much of his research at the Rutherford Appleton Laboratory in Oxfordshire.**

Lockwood has observed a sustained decline in the sun`s activity. Indeed he believes that the sun's activity is in free fall. Solar activity is declining faster than at any time in the past 10 thousand years according to Mike Lockwood, professor of space environmental physics at Reading University.

British scientist Mike Lockwood from the Rutherford Appleton Laboratory believes that solar activity affects our jet stream weather patterns. The jet stream is a band of incredibly fast moving westerly winds high up in the atmosphere which circle around the pole.

It can feature winds of up to 200 knots (230 mph) and these winds tend to guide wet and windy weather systems which come via the Atlantic.

The jet stream moves around and its position can have a big impact on weather here in the UK. If the jet is over the UK or just to the south, we tend to get a lot of wet and windy conditions as it brings weather systems straight to us.

The floods in the British Isles of 2014/15 were caused by a powerful jet stream. Cold easterly winds from Siberia are influenced by low sunspot activity. In February 2018 an excited press announced that the Siberian "beast from the east" was about to bring freezing blizzards of sleet and snow to Great Britain!

The Dalton minimum was a cool climate sunspot cycle from 1790 to 1830 discovered by the astronomer Jon Dalton and his wife Annie Dalton. Another low sunspot cycle was known as the Maunder Minimum that took place from 1645 to 1715.

Let us not underestimate the biting cold of the Maunder Minimum which was bitterly hostile to life. The sunspot minimum happened at the same time that weather in Northern America and Europe became unusually icy and cold. The Maunder Minimum occurred in the 17th century and lasted around 70 years.

During this time Londoners enjoyed skating upon the River Thames. The citizens that lived in 17th century Europe survived these cold winters, without the heating and insulation technology that we are fortunate to have today.

If the next solar activity minimum does affect the weather on Earth, perhaps it will not be so unpleasant for Londoners. However if another little ice age were to morph into a great ice age things might not look so rosy.

The Maunder Minimum was studied by the astronomer John A. Eddy who was a solar astronomer. Eddy demonstrated that our sun is not a constant star with a regular cycle but rather one that has periods of anomaly and variation. In

1976, the astronomer Dr. Eddy published an article in the journal *Science* in which he confirmed the speculative observations of 19th-century astronomers.

Eddy noted that from 1645 to 1715, the surface of the Sun was inordinately calm. The sun's magnetic storms which are indicated by sunspots were peculiarly absent. "I have re-examined the contemporary reports and new evidence which has come to light since Maunder's time and conclude that this 70-year period was indeed a time when solar activity all but stopped," Eddy wrote.

Is it really possible that a lack of sunspots could have caused such a drop in the temperature in Great Britain? A sunspot is a cooler area on the surface of the sun in the photosphere that appears dark. There appears to be a correlation between the number of sunspots and solar radiation. Sunspots have a hypothesised effect on our climate and sunspots also provide useful information for space weather forecasts that enable the safety of satellites to be monitored.

The future predicted activity of the Sun in the coming decades has been likened to the Maunder Minimum. There was also another cooling period after the Medieval Warm period during the five centuries long period known as the Dark Ages.

So it appears that there have been quite a few cool periods in the past. It looks as though we may be heading towards another such cool climate event if the solar physicists are correct in their predictions about declining solar activity.

In the not too distant future the River Thames might once more freeze over. In days gone by the River Thames was the scene of frost fairs and market stalls were set up on the icy waters. This could be a reality once more for the citizens of London.

Perhaps an ice rink or two may also appear on the River Thames. Recent structural and engineering changes to the London bridges perhaps make it less likely that the River Thames will freeze over since it now flows faster. So maybe we will not live to enjoy the ironic spectacle of our elected politicians gaily skating on the River Thames!

With all of the talk about man-made global warming one would think that humans are in control of the climate and that our Sun has a mere peripheral role. Indeed our star that is powered by thermonuclear fusion has been relegated to a bystander role in the warming of our planet. This is plainly nonsense.

I recall a member of the audience in an Oxford talk given by global warming author Mark lynas about the climate. He politely raised his hand while tentatively enquiring about the role of the Sun in our climate?

Was the author really sure that our carbon dioxide emissions were the main driver of the climate, he nervously asked. Never a person to be fazed by an awkward question the confident author brushed the topic aside like an annoying gnat buzzing around his person.

The Sun it seems is not that important at all as a driver of climate, he opined. Tides will rise and flat Holland`s colourful tulip farms would be washed away under a tsunami caused by carbon dioxide induced global warming. It seems it was not the Sun keeping us warm after all but the warming greenhouse emissions from our coal fires.

Not everyone was entirely happy with the downplaying of the Sun`s role in climatic variables , but on the whole the audience left the Oxford talk feeling suitably entertained and satisfied with their outing.

The book promotional talk had presented us with an agreeable frisson of dangerous calamity as well as the prospect of a balmy Bermuda like climate replacing the boring grey skies of Great Britain. Plus there had been nice slides to look at and very comfy plush leather chairs to lounge on in the Turl Street club.

However most of the audience left the talk endowed with a healthy degree of cynicism. That is not to say that I do not agree that it might be dreadful for our entire planet to warm by six degrees. However the opposite scenario of a global cooling by minus six degrees would be equally horrific and bring a major ice age to the Northern Hemisphere.

Indeed we are only five degrees away from entering an ice age right now and there are some worrying signs that our sun may be going into a period of hibernation.

In 1990 NASA and the European Space Agency joined forces to send a satellite to orbit the sun. This robot satellite was called Ulysses and provided some unique data about the sun as it made three complete orbits before it was decommissioned in 2009. The robotic probe was also collecting data about the heliosphere which is the entire region of our solar system that is dominated by the sun`s energy.

The solar wind extends right to the far edge of our solar system beyond Pluto where it eventually pauses at it encounters interstellar space. At this junction it becomes known as the heliopause.

The heliopause arises when the solar wind has become too weak to counteract the interstellar medium. There is a large increase of cosmic ray influx at the heliopause due to the weakness of the solar wind. Lest my readers start to yawn I should explain that all of this is very important for our climate here on Earth.

A very interesting finding was that the solar wind was measured as becoming progressively weaker during the twenty year mission.

The magnetosphere is crucial to deflect various nasties coming at us from deep space. These nasties include cosmic rays that are highly radioactive. These rays are mutagenic particles that emanate from the Galaxy. Cosmic rays are present at a high altitude in Earth's upper atmosphere.

Passengers in high altitude aircraft may be at risk if they are frequent fliers or are pregnant. However a healthy buoyant solar wind is able to deflect most of the harmful galactic cosmic rays away from Earth`s upper atmosphere.

In 2008 it was reported that the solar wind was at its weakest strength since recordings had begun in 1969. The solar wind had declined in strength by 20 percent. One of the principal investigators for Ulysses was Dave McComas who is based in San Antonio, Texas. McComas was overseeing a solar wind sensor aboard Ulysses called SWOOPS. He was shocked to record such a large drop in the solar wind strength.

As the mission was uncovering a lot of interesting data you would have thought that NASA would continue to fund this worthy mission. Sadly this was not the case and the funding was withdrawn. Perhaps the funding was diverted to study carbon dioxide levels back on Earth!

This decision is extremely unfortunate as if the solar levels continue on a downward trajectory it may have important repercussion here on Earth.

The repercussions on our climate of a quiescent sun may turn out to be far worse than any hypothetical anthropogenic warming. This winding down of our sun`s strength may be the warning sign that we are soon to enter into a new ice age.

This conjecture is given further weight by the fact that cosmic rays are thought to influence cloud formation on planet Earth. A weaker solar wind allows more of these galactic cosmic rays to penetrate our atmosphere.

Thus when the cosmic ray flux increases due to a weakening solar wind there is the potential for more clouds to form. The whiteness of the clouds in turn may provide a greater albedo effect as the sun's rays bounce back into cold space. Thus there is feedback loop whereby a weakening solar wind may indirectly lead to a lowering of Earth's temperatures.

This idea was fully explored by Nigel Calder and Henrik Svensmark in their excellent book "Chilling Stars, a new theory of Climate Change". The former editor of New Scientist, Nigel Calder, makes a strong case in this book for the sun being the main driver of climatic variables as opposed to carbon dioxide.

The sun's heliosphere is created by the solar wind and it is now drastically is shrinking. The heliosphere reaches to the very outer reach of our solar system. The heliosphere is protecting our solar system from the high intensity cosmic radiation from outer space.

This heliosphere is generated by electrically charged particles travelling at speeds of a million miles an hour from the sun. At the far reaches of our solar system a shock wave forms that deflects the interstellar radiation.

The heliospheric solar wind has been measured as being 20 per cent less dense by the Ulysses mission. Since the solar wind is no longer inflating the entire solar system heliosphere there is much less shielding from cosmic rays.

This is very worrying as there has been a lot of research by Henrik Svensmark showing that cosmic rays may lower global temperatures. The cooling influence of increasing cosmic rays on our climate will be discussed in a later chapter. The heliosphere is vital to life on Earth and without it life would be impossible here.

Yet despite its importance to our existence a decision was made to withdraw funding for the Ulysses shrinking heliosphere study!

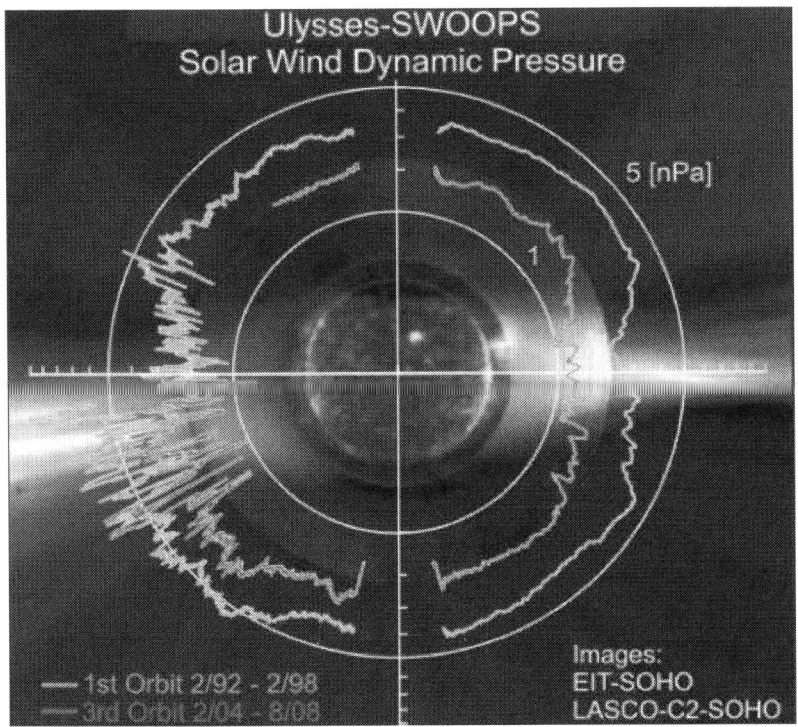

The Ulysses Mission funded by NASA and ESA shows the solar wind is cooler and less dense.

Ulysses also discovered that dust coming into the Solar System from deep space was 30 times more abundant than previously expected.

This space dust could also exacerbate the trend for a new ice age as the ultra fine micron particle dust veil reflects light back into cold space. The unpublished data from the abandoned Ulysses project found that the number of cosmic ray particles jumped by 20 per cent in our upper atmosphere. This is a huge increase of a deadly particle. The Ulysses mission also found that the sun`s underlying magnetic field has been weakening by around 30 percent since the 1960`s.

In 2007–2008 *Ulysses* determined that the magnetic field emanating from the Sun's poles is much weaker than previously observed (NASA briefing 2008). A weakening of the magnetic field shrinks the heliosphere emanating from the sun enabling more cosmic rays to enter our atmosphere.

Ulysses discovered that the Sun's magnetic field interacts with the Solar

System in a more complex fashion than previously assumed.

   Since this worthwhile mission was rashly halted in 2009 we can only guess as to what is now happening to the solar wind. This shrinking of our the heliosphere would mean that any future voyager missions would be able to reach the region outside our solar system that is known as interstellar space in a shorter time.

   In other words the freezing life threatening cold region of intergalactic space is drawing ever nearer to our planet that is presently thriving happily in the Goldilocks zone!

   The magnetic fields of both the Sun and the Earth are thought to be generated by similar "dynamo" processes that involve rotating conducting fluid. The field is generated by molten iron in the case of the Earth and hot ionized gases in the Sun.

The Wilcox Solar Observatory has observed the sun`s magnetic field since 1975. The data from the observatory show that the sun`s two hemispheres are strangely out of synch at times. Intriguingly changes in the sun`s magnetic field affect lightning strikes here on Earth!

The Sun`s magnetic field can warp Earth`s magnetic field. This in turn leads to increases in cosmic rays that precipitate thunderstorms and lightning. The seeding of thunder clouds by cosmic rays creates lightning bolts of electrical energy.

The high energy particles called galactic cosmic rays provide the link that lets the current flow into a lightning bolt. The sun's magnetic field impacts Earth's magnetic field in a way that triggers electrical thunderstorms. A single cosmic ray is a proton that has energies a million times higher than anything produced in the Large Hadron Collider at Cern in Switzerland.

The galactic cosmic rays provide a wire-like conducting channel of ionisation that charges lightning bolts. Lightning strikes here on earth are triggered by energetic particles brought via the solar wind. Astrophysicists have observed that cosmic rays can affect weather on Earth.

The link between the Sun's activity and thunderstorms can provide a useful tool for predicting our weather.

So when there is a thunderstorm blame the sun for a magnetic field disturbance!

The frequency of lightning strikes follows regular patterns that match the rotation of the Sun`s magnetic field.

David Hathaway of NASA Marshall Space Flight Centre and Matthew Penn of the National Solar Observatory have also found a decline in solar activity.

The team presented their unexpected findings at the July 2013 meeting of the American Society Solar Physics Division. Hathaway observed a weakening of the solar cycle 24. This was a surprising finding as in 2009 Hathaway thought that the future solar cycle 24 would remain strong and buoyant.

The Russian scientists Zharkova and Popova have recently replicated this seminal 2013 American study of diminishing sunspots.

The Sun has recently put on its weakest performance for one hundred years according to Hathaway. This rapid powering down is extremely worrying.

Could this data be warning us of a major glaciation event?

Cycle 24 is the weakest for 100 years, D. Hathaway, NASA

Matthew Penn came up with a catastrophic hypothesis to account for the data. Penn speculates that the sunspot cycle might die completely. His predictions are based on the weakening magnetic field within the sunspots. David Hathaway based his measurements of the Sun's polar field and the *meridional flow* which is the flow of magnetic flux from the Sun's equator to the poles.

  A stronger flow would help strengthen weak fields, but meridional flows have been completely absent in cycle 24. As far back as 2008 it was observed that there were 266 days without any sunspots! Both Hathaway and Penn expect the coming solar cycles to be the weakest recorded. Worryingly David Hathaway thinks that the last Maunder Minimum was a catastrophic event causing mass starvation.

Matthew Penn and William Livingston predict sunspots may vanish when the magnetic field strength falls below 1500 gauss.

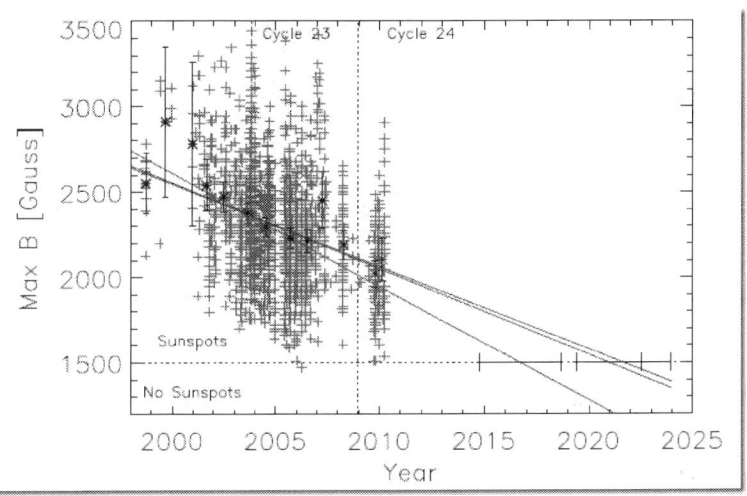

Penn and Livingston 2010

Shows the field strength declining

The astrophysicists made a linear extrapolation of the magnetic field trends. This suggested that the threshold of 1500 Gauss would be reached by the year 2017 (Penn and Livingston 2010).

As you can see in the second diagram the projected solar cycle 25 shows a collapse of sunspots and perhaps will mark the start of a major ice age!

While some scientists are debating whether we will see a return of the mini ice age weather patterns, they may be missing the huge elephant which is the next major ice age. Lockwood and his colleagues are wondering whether the decline will become the first "grand solar minimum" for four centuries.

During a grand minimum the normal 11-year solar cycle is suppressed and the sun has virtually no **sunspots** for several decades. There should have been a peak in the number of sunspots, but it didn't happen. Professor Lockwood thinks there is a 25 per cent probability of Maunder Minimum conditions when there were no recorded sunspots for 70 years!

The National solar Observatory in Tucson Arizona has recorded a drop in magnetic sunspot activity since 1995. William Livingston and his colleague Matthew Penn have recorded a slide in sunspot magnetic fields for which there is no explanation.

The Solar and Heliospheric Observatory, SOHO, mission has

recorded a drop in the actual output of the sun by 0.015 per cent.

This fall in solar irradiance was measured by the Virgo instrument. This may sound small but actually depicts a huge fall in solar output. A fall in output actually suggests that the sun may be shrinking! The amount of heat the sun gifts us here on planet Earth depends on the second power of the solar diameter.

Therefore a minuscule change in diameter could throw the Earth into an ice age. This concept of a shrinking sun was explored in the film *Sunshine* where a team of scientists embark on a perilous journey to the sun in the year

2057. Their aim is to reignite the dying sun with a nuclear bomb!

Apart from the data provided by the Ulysses satellite there has been more recent data coming in from solar physicists regarding the sun's activity.

A recent study by Professor Valentina Zharkova at the Wilcox solar observatory observed that our sun is reverting to a less active sunspot phase comparable to the low sunspot number observed during the Maunder and Dalton Minimum.

Zharkova thinks that the next sunspot minimum will last for 30 years. The cautious astronomer predicts that the climate might become cooler in Great Britain. "The conditions during this next predicted minimum will be chilly. "It will be cold, but it will not be this ice age when everything is freezing like in the Hollywood Day After Tomorrow films," Zharkova says!

There are some scientists who believe that something far worse may be about to happen! Zharkova`s team monitored the Sun's background magnetic field which causes solar features like sunspots. After analysing the solar data Zharkova's team noticed something that no one had observed before.

It was observed that the Sun produces its magnetic waves in pairs. Previously researchers had thought that there was only a single source of magnetic waves in the Sun, but the new groundbreaking evidence suggested two sources.

The team used these observations to predict how the Sun's magnetic field would change in the future. This is how the team predicted the new Maunder like solar conditions that will arrive in the year 2030.

The conditions will thereafter continue to get worse. During the solar minimum, the intensity of solar radiation will be reduced dramatically. So we will have less heat coming into the atmosphere, which will in turn reduce the global temperature. **Will this be the start of our overdue ice age?**

Zharkova and her colleagues use a technique called principal component analysis of the magnetic field. The researchers analysed magnetograms for three cycles of solar activity by applying principal component analysis.

This reduces the data dimensionality and noise to identify waves with the largest contribution. This method can be compared with the decomposition of white light on the rainbow prism detecting waves of different frequencies. This method reveals that the magnetic waves in the Sun are generated in pairs (Zharkova et al, 2012, MNRAS).

They observations were recorded from the Wilcox Solar Observatory in California. Zharkova`s team examined three solar cycles of magnetic field activity, covering the period from 1976-2008.

They compared their predictions of temperature to average sunspot numbers which are a strong marker of solar activity. The predictions and observations closely matched. Looking ahead to the next solar cycles, the model predicts that the pair of waves increasingly offset during Cycle 25. The Russian scientist calculated the summary curve linked to the variations of sunspot number.

This solar cycle 25 peaks in the year 2022. During Cycle 26, which covers the decade from 2030-2040, the two waves will become exactly out of synch. This phase is predicted to cause a significant reduction in solar activity. This solar cycle is the start of our mini ice age cycle. When there is full phase separation, we have the very cold conditions last seen during the Maunder minimum, 370 years ago.

Another astronomer, Dr. Helen Popova, agrees with the sunspot theory. She also spoke at the North Wales astronomy conference in Llandudno in 2015. She has developed a similar mathematical model of the Sun`s magnetic activity. The model also indicates a reduction in sunspots during the future solar sunspot minimum that could lead to a cooling of the Earth`s atmosphere. Popova agrees that the principal component pair is responsible for the variations of a dipole field of the Sun.

The magnetic waves are assumed to originate in two different layers in the sun (Popova et al, 2013). Both scientists correctly predicted that sunspot magnetic activity would decrease in the present day solar cycle 24. This forecast of low sunspot activity has proven to be accurate in the year 2018.

Our present day cycle has been the quietest for over a century. This quiescence could be an ominous sign of things to come (Zharkova et al 2015).

The Royal Astronomical Society (RAS) concurs with the Russian solar physicists and predicted that solar activity will fall by as much as 60% in the 2030`s to 'mini ice age' levels.

A new model of the Sun's solar cycle is producing unprecedentedly accurate predictions of irregularities within the Sun's 11-year heartbeat.

The model draws on dynamo effects in two layers of the Sun, one close to the surface and one deep within its convection zone. Solar cycle 25 will take place in the years 2019 – 2030 and solar cycle 26 takes place in the years 2030-2040. The dynamo model of the Sun was originally first observed by Mausumo Dikpati` s team in 2004.

The RAS model of the sun confirms that it is driven by a double dynamo (July 9, 2015 Royal Astronomical

Society). **The RAS agrees that the waves will become fully separated in opposite hemispheres in cycle 26 and thus have little chance of interacting and producing sunspots.**

This will lead to a sharp decline in solar activity in years 2030-2040 comparable with the conditions existed previously during the Maunder minimum in the XVII century. During this freezing and impoverished time there were only about 50-70 sunspots observed instead of the usual 40-50 thousand.

This is a massive drop in numbers that will lead to a reduction of the solar irradiance by 3W/m² according to solar physicists. This reduction in solar input of 3 watts per meter squared is actually rather large when one considers that the IPCC say that carbon dioxide will manage to somehow heat Earth by 1.4 watts per meter squared! If these figures are correct then mankind could be in for a nasty shock as the temperatures plummet in the Northern Hemisphere. This reduction in sunspots could lead to a new mini ice age. This predicted solar irradiance reduction might also be exacerbated by the increasing cosmic radiation and a global dimming that is caused by our polluted skies and volcanoes.

Together the many contributing factors could amplify the trend for cooling in a deadly cooling feedback loop. Such a large reduction in solar radiance far outstrips any insulation reduction from a Milankovitch cycle. Therefore this prediction is rather worrying to say the least!

If the theories about the impact of solar activity on the climate are correct, then this sunspot minimum will lead to a significant cooling, similar to the one that occurred during the Maunder Minimum.

To reiterate, the Maunder Minimum coincided with the coldest phase of the 500 year period known as the "Little Ice Age" which began in 1315.

This cold period was preceded by a medieval warm period. This warmth lasted from 900 to 1315 A.D and resulted in a flourishing prosperous era of enormous productivity and great Cathedral building. Then in 1315 the balmy climate suddenly disappeared in Northern Europe and crops failed after snow and torrential rains weakened them.

This sudden change in the climate was followed by a great famine in the years 1315-1317. The Little Ice Age continued for 500 years until it ended around 1850.The foul and thunderstorm ridden weather was sometimes blamed on witches who were accused of brewing up diabolical storms! Temperatures dropped by ten degrees and crops had become waterlogged.

Every devastating hail storm was blamed on sorcery and witchcraft, since the science of meteorology was unknown. "In 1445, was a very strong hail and wind, as never seen before, did great damage; many women, said to have made the hail were burned as witches according to the law" (Behringer 1999).

The Astronomer, William Herschel, tracked the price of wheat and bread and how these varied with sunspot activity. The astronomer found that fewer sunspots resulted in lower yields of wheat.

During the Maunder Minimum there was often heavy rainfall during the summer months that made crops water logged. Millions of people died from starvation during the coldest years which were from 1645 to 1720. Think of our very wet summer in 2012 in Great Britain and this might give an idea of how a mini ice age summer would have ruined crop yields.

These days there is a tendency to equate floods and stormy weather with a manmade warming. Yet the evidence points to this pattern of very wet stormy weather as being prevalent during the cold Little Ice Age. During this period there were very cold wet winters in Europe and North America. Waterlogged crops resulted in famine.

The 500 year long little ice age culminated in the cold Maunder

Minimum when the Thames and Danube Rivers froze. The Moscow River was covered by ice and Greenland covered in glaciers in the 17th century. During this period, there were only about 50 sunspots instead of the usual 40-50 thousand sunspots which is a huge drop in numbers.

   The Sun has its own magnetic field. The amplitude and spatial configuration of the magnetic field vary with time. This results in changes of intensity of plasma flows coming from the Sun, and the number of sunspots on the Sun's surface.

   The number of sunspots on the Sun's surface has a cyclic structure that varies every 11 years. This cycle is indicated by the analysis of carbon-14 and beryllium-10, glacier isotopes. There are several solar cycles with different periods and properties. As well as the 11 year sunspot cycle there is thought to be a 90 year cycle and a 206 year cycle.

It seems that our Sun is far from stable and highly prone to variation. NASA and the University of Arizona measured magnetic-field measurements 120,000 miles beneath the sun's surface. Their findings also suggest that solar Cycle 25, due in 2020, will be a great deal weaker still. Solar cycle 26 which is arriving in the year 2030 is expected to be the smallest in over 300 years. As for solar cycle 27 one can only speculate how cold it might be if the sun`s dynamo does not recover!

It is interesting to also speculate as to the cause of the simultaneous decline in our Sun`s magnetic field with the Earth`s magnetic field. Could the two declines in field strength be somehow connected and be a terrible warning of our impending ice age? This decline could coincide with the dawn of a new mini ice age or worse.

We could experience a dramatically fast transition to an ice age if the pollen and plant records are correct. Pollen records show how plants changed from warmth loving species to cold weather varieties in a very short time frame. A variable output star like the Sun could literally become dim. We could wake up one day in Great Britain to find our sun looks eerily pale and wan at the dawn of a new ice age.

The solar cycle that we really need to look out for is solar cycle 26. This cycle begins in the year 2030. This could be the year we notice a return to very severe cold weather conditions last seen in the 17th century when the River Thames would freeze.

Imagine how surprised our politicians would be when they look out of the Houses of Parliament onto a frozen river. Especially imagine the reaction of the politicians who were involved in climate legislation to save carbon emissions to prevent a rise in temperatures! Instead of the predicted warming, there will be a deep freeze in the middle of this century!

Since solar cycle 26 is being heralded as the harbinger of a dramatic drop in temperature it may get even worse by the year 2050. Some of us may live to see the dawn of a huge glacial inception that heralds the dawn of our major overdue ice age.

All fears of a global warming will be long forgotten as we struggle to adapt to a massive ice age. A major ice age is far worse than a mini ice age lasting a few decades, as it usually lasts for at least 90, 000 years!

Pensioners may also start to die in increasing numbers as the cold winds bite. The elderly are more vulnerable to freezing temperatures and already the winter mortality rate is unacceptably high in Great Britain. Life in a freezing Great Britain may come as a nasty shock. Pensioners might be wise to consider migrating to warmer Southern climes such as the Spanish Costas, though they too might succumb to the ice age.

Let us hope we will not end up suddenly frozen like the woolly mammoths found with food still in their mouths as they suddenly froze to death. No one knows for sure why the mammoths and mastodons died out suddenly overnight while eating their dinner.

Millions of mammoths have been found buried in permafrost and the indications are they possibly could have frozen to death instantly as many were still standing.

Many of the deep frozen mammoths had broken bones and this could have been caused by gigantic hailstones, during an ice storm that killed them instantly. It is unlikely that the mammoths were eaten by hunter gatherers as their remains were found in very unnatural positions. The suspicion is that they all died instantly probably in a giant ice storm with hail the size of golf balls.

We have to consider the awful possibility that a major climatic upheaval could result in a mass extinction event. Could an ice age come on suddenly within months as has been suggested?

Could this coming cycle of solar sunspot quiescence herald the dawn of a major ice age unlike anything that mankind has ever seen? Cycle 26 may be the trigger for the inception of our overdue great ice age that arrives at the end of every interglacial.

This deadly ice age is now due to begin according to data from the geologic record. Since we are now overdue a major ice age, this solar sunspot cycle may herald the dawn of a major ice age that just happens to commence along with the expected mini ice age. A major ice age will be up to 30 times colder than a mini ice age event such as that of the Maunder Minimum!

Our Sun may not be a normal star that shines and irradiates in a homogeneous unchanging fashion. The Sun instead may vary in its luminosity. It might fluctuate in a similar way to variable stars known as Cepheids.

These Cepheid stars fluctuate periodically in a way that depends on mass and luminosity. Our Sun has many phases and cycles and is chronically unstable. The Sun is almost human like in waking up and becoming fully alert and then falling asleep and becoming dormant. Maybe the idea of the Sun becoming weak and faint is not so far-fetched after all.

Some scientists take this concept of a variable star to a whole new level. They believe that the Sun is affected by primer fields from interstellar space. When the primer fields become inactive the Earth's climate can become 40 times colder than it is at present! Scientists are convinced that the Sun's primer fields are showing signs of a rapid decline.

This will plummet us into major ice age conditions by the year 2050. This will be far colder than a mini ice age.

Not everyone agrees with the primer field theory of plasma cosmology. However the declining solar output predicted does seem to coincide with the accepted Ulysses data on measured declining solar winds.

Data from the Ulysses solar mission suggest that a catastrophic fall in the Sun's output will have occurred by the year 2050. If the trajectory continues then it is possible that a cut -off point of no solar recovery will be crossed around the year 2040.

After the year 2040, the projected graph of diminishing solar heliospheric wind shows that our Sun becomes comparable to a white dwarf star in output!

Of course he does not really mean that our sun will become like a white dwarf star as this scenario is not expected for another six billion years when our Sun runs out of fuel! However this scientist thinks that the sun`s strength will diminish and become very weak.

This may sound very fanciful and fantastic even, and yet there is plenty of evidence that our Sun may be a variable star from the sunspot cycle. As such there is no reason why its output should not vary and become very weak. It is said that in the very distant epochs of our planet's history the sun used to shine dimly in the earliest epochs of the Hadean and the Archean eons.

4.5 billion years ago, our Sun was 30% fainter than it is today and Earth should have been frozen solid, but it wasn't. This problem was coined as the "Faint Sun Paradox" by the charismatic astronomer Carl Sagan. It seems that Earth is remarkably resilient and that life will survive the harshest conditions (Sagan and Mullen 1972).

A fainter sun may seem an outlandish theory but it is consistent with a burgeoning theory called the electric universe. The electric universe theory turns accepted dogma completely on its head. In this type of universe it seems that unusual things happen. These unusual events include our reliable life giving sun switching off its power output so that it becomes so insipid and pale.

Some solar physicists believe that the central nuclear furnace may not burn constantly but fluctuate, in a similar way to a thermostat. The electric universe theory that says our Sun is a plasma star and burns only on the surface.

These theorists believe that the Sun is cooler on the inside than on the outside. The electric theory presumes there is no thermonuclear reaction taking place inside our Sun. This might be why sunspots appear dark in the space telescopes, as the core of the Sun is empty.

   This is contrast to the conventional theory of how our Sun works, burning hydrogen for another 5 to 6 billion years before running out of fuel. The Sun will then evolve firstly into a red giant and then a white dwarf. Phew! That is a lot more reassuring to hear. 5 billion years is certainly a lot more time for us to enjoy our beloved sunshine than a mere 35 years. A white dwarf analogy is perhaps taking things a bit too far in the attempt to explain the Sun`s predicted diminishing output.

   It is deduced that sunspots are dark since there is nothing inside the Sun at all. The Sun might be an empty hollow globe with all the activity taking place only on its surface. This fluctuation may be in response to conditions in the surrounding galaxy.

The idea that there is no nuclear reaction at all occurring at the centre of the sun is certainly radical and alarming. This electric universe theory is in stark contrast to the conventional and accepted model of how our Sun works.

This innovative theory of an electric universe could theoretically be used to explain the sudden onset of a major ice age event. The Sun`s output diminishes to such an extent that the Earth almost instantly becomes frozen. This ice age will then last for around 100, 0000 years before the Sun somehow kicks starts itself back into life and the solar output once more increases.

It is certainly the most incredible theory, and if this electric universe theory is correct then mankind could one day see our Sun change in luminosity before our very eyes. One day we may wake up and look at the sky and see that our sun has changed forever in our lifetime. No longer will it burn brightly and with cheery warmth. Instead there will be a pale ghostly globe that is almost moon like in our eerily cold skies!

According to the electric universe theory, the Sun`s primer fields are simultaneously powering down as unusual intergalactic changes are taking place. Once a threshold is crossed of a diminishing solar output the Sun may not recover its vitality. The point of no return for a recovery of the sun`s magnetic dynamo is projected to be around the years 2035 to 2040. Then we will be tipped once more into our full ice age lasting 100, 000 years.

There can be no doubt that our universe is brimming with electrical phenomena such as sprites. Scientists at the University of Toronto have discovered a strong electric current in space that is two billion light years from Earth. Philipp Kronberg said that this space lightning electric current was found near galaxy 3C303, and is equal to about 1 trillion lightning bolts (New Scientist 2011).

Findings such as these do tend to corroborate an electric universe. This idea is not a new crackpot theory and has actually been around since the year 1903 when George Woodward Warder wrote a book saying that the universe is a vast electric organism.

There is no doubt that this electric universe theory stimulates an enquiring mind to look at the universe in a different light.

Electric universe theory states that the chaos of Brownian motion produces the high temperatures we see in the solar corona. The idea that our Sun is not powered by fusion from its core, but somehow draws energy from its galactic environment is certainly unusual.

There is no doubt that our universe is full of exciting electric phenomena such as aurora, lightning strikes and sprites which are a cold plasma artefact. Computer simulations have demonstrated that the motion of the spiral galaxy can be achieved through nothing other than interactions of electric currents in plasma. This theory allegedly explains why 95 per cent of the matter is supposedly missing in our universe that is the missing *dark matter*.

However the electric universe theory has been discounted by mainstream science as the concept challenges most of mainstream cosmology, and even gets rid of the big bang altogether! It also tries to get rid of the concept of gravity and so is considered somewhat heretical.

There are however reasons to be concerned about our pithy knowledge of the Sun`s workings. There is plentiful evidence that our Sun is a variable star. This group consists of several kinds of pulsating stars all found on the instability strip, that swell and shrink very regularly.

The nuclear reactions taking place in the Sun are supposed to produce neutrinos. According to the standard model the Sun should be emitting vast quantities of neutrinos. However these hypothetical particles have proved elusive and they may be an invention to balance the books for the theory of supersymmetry.

The tiny fraction of detected neutrinos do not account for the present solar theoretical model. So we must ask ourselves the question, do we really know what is going on inside the Sun?

A scientist named Ernst Opik thought that ice ages came when the Sun`s core became swollen and did not convect the heat as efficiently to the outer layer. However it is all speculation since we really do not know exactly what is happening in the core. The theory that neutrinos are produced by thermonuclear reactions at the core may be completely wrong. This possibly incorrect model of the Sun could account for the lack of neutrinos detected to date.

Or perhaps the missing neutrinos could be a warning sign that the Sun is slowing down and gearing up for an ice age. The very small amount of neutrinos allegedly detected might imply that the Sun is far less hot than we think.

As a result some solar physicists are questioning the conventional theories about the Sun. Or there is the remote possibility that the lack of neutrinos could mean that the Sun is sick and not producing enough reactions in its core. This is a very worrying idea as it might imply the Sun is dying!

To account for the missing neutrinos some astrophysicists have invented the WIMP, which is a weakly interacting massive particle. American physicists believe there in only one WIMP for every hundred billion particles inside the Sun. WIMPS are said to collide with protons bringing heat from the inner core to the outer core, before arriving to Earth. WIMPS can therefore possibly explain how Sun`s heat gets to Earth and they may account for the missing neutrinos.

If we really understood the nuclear fusion processes taking place inside the sun then perhaps we would have mastered thermonuclear fusion by now. This is plainly not the case as the long running projects at ITER (International Thermonuclear Experimental Reactor) and JET (Joint European Torus) in Oxfordshire have shown. So far the hugely expensive project at Culham in Oxfordshire that uses super-heated plasma has only produced enough energy to boil one kettle worth of energy!

In other words the expensive project has so far failed to deliver the dream of fusion power. I attended a very interesting meeting once at Culham with my friend an Italian plasma scientist. The project is a good example of international collaboration amongst scientists and no doubt some interesting findings are being made along the way.

   I do believe that the present day approach to the fusion process must be wrong. This may be due to the fact that it is based upon an incorrect model of how the Sun works. The project at JET is creating superheated plasma that is hotter than the Sun! This is clearly a foolish and not to mention a vastly expensive approach. The energy output achieved so far from the expensive experiment is just about enough to boil a single kettle as the joke goes. This makes for a very expensive cup of tea or coffee!!

   Just a smidgeon of common sense will tell us that we need to explore a cheap economic power source and the present nuclear fusion experiment is not able to provide this. If we are heading for an ice age of some description we need to expand our power supply as our population increases and more new homes are built.

In case anyone is confused at this point let me reiterate that nuclear *fusion* power is preferable to nuclear *fission* power. Fission power can lead to dangerous radiation leaks as happened in Chernobyl, Windscale, Fukushima and Three Mile Island to name just a few nuclear power accidents. Nuclear fusion power which is considered safer has been the Holy Grail quest for energy for a long time now since the 1950`s.

At one point a lot of excitement was generated when two scientists became convinced that they had accidentally stumbled upon cold fusion. In 1989, chemists Stanley Pons and Martin Fleischmann made headlines with claims that they had produced fusion at room temperature.

The chemists even published a paper about the accidental discovery. The chemists claimed that their test tube experiment had produced anomalous heat and that they had found small amounts of nuclear by products such as neutrons and tritium. It must have been quite an exciting day in the lab!

Nonetheless the table top experiment was deemed to be a fluke and many scientists doubted whether any nuclear by products had really been detected.

Countless attempts to replicate the exciting finding since by scores of hopeful scientists have all proved fruitless.

It looks as if the cold fusion reaction incident was a one off and the idea of cold fusion has since been relegated to the archives of oblivion. So once again the focus turned to hot thermonuclear fusion. This also looks like another red herring and has been similarly unsuccessful.

The researchers at JET claim that higher outputs of energy are being achieved recently and that they are slowly on the road to success. This belief seems somewhat overly optimistic. Jet is planning to use Tritium and deuterium plasmas for 2018. The reactions taking place on the Sun may have intergalactic influences which may be impossible to replicate on this Earth in a humble Torus shaped tokamak.

The world`s largest tokamak magnetic confinement ring is being built in France. This project is known as ITER (International thermonuclear Experimental Reactor). It will be finished in 2020 and is hoped to produce 500 mega watts of energy.

This fusion reactor is being constructed in a French town named Saint Paul les Durance in Cadarache. China is also experimenting with this concept and is working on a China Fusion Engineering Test Reactor (CFETR).

Really at this stage we should be looking at projects that deliver gigawatts worth of energy as opposed to mere paltry megawatts. I am tempted to suggest that a cyclist pedalling on a self sufficiency type hybrid bike would produce more useful energy than these astronomically expensive attempts at fusion power. Incidentally a new bicycle pedal powered gadget has been invented for an Indian company by Manoj Bhargava. This bike can provide 24 hours of electricity for a rural household.

This device could have a major impact in Indian rural areas that are not supplied with electricity. These bikes are known as free electric bikes. It is hoped that they will make a vast difference to the lives of many who have no access to electricity.

It is planned to distribute thousands of these bikes in India. This concept shows how microgeneration of energy can be achieved in a way that creates no pollution whatsoever (Derek Markham 2015).

The microgeneration approach to energy production would not be a feasible means to provide the large scale amounts of electricity needed to run industry and big cities such as London. I can hardly imagine our City bankers pedalling furiously instead of sitting at their desks while making deals with stocks and hedge funds! Still who knows what the future holds? Perhaps one day this may actually happen if there is a national power shortage as predicted by OFGEM.

Our energy hungry society needs to explore the larger macrogeneration projects such as JET even if they are so far proving futile. To this end the plasma scientists need to start examining their models to align with those of solar researchers who are questioning how the Sun works.

However if the fundamental theory of how the Sun produces heat is fundamentally flawed then it may be impossible to achieve success using superheated plasmas. The fusion reaction may not take place internally in the Sun at all but on the surface of the Sun. However other scientists point out that the sunspots may just appear dark in contrast to the surrounding brilliant glare of the Sun. Therefore we have some solar physicists that believe the Sun is cooler internally.

The mainstream view is that our Sun is much hotter at the core as this is where the thermonuclear fusion reaction is taking place. The converse theory of a cooler central core is a highly speculative theory but certainly we should keep an open mind.

This theory might also help explain the missing neutrinos that are proving so elusive to capture here on Earth. It also explains why the heat from the sun increases further away from the surface around the corona. This cool core hypothesis aligns with the electric plasma theory of the universe.

The notion that solar magnetic activity affects the climate, appeared long ago. It is known, for example, that a change in the total quantity of the electromagnetic radiation by only 1% can result in a noticeable change in the temperature distribution and air flow all over the Earth. Ultraviolet rays also cause a photochemical effect, which leads to the formation of ozone.

The flow of ultraviolet radiation increases sharply during chromospheric flares in the Sun. Ozone, which absorbs the Sun's rays, is heated and it affects the air currents in the lower layers of the atmosphere and, consequently, the weather. Powerful emissions which can reach the Earth's surface arise periodically during high solar activity. They can move in complex trajectories, causing aurorae, geomagnetic storms and disturbances of radio communication.

In addition, the solar activity affects the intensity of fluxes of galactic cosmic rays. Another interesting theory has suggested that the Sun is presently immersed in an intergalactic cloud of hydrogen and helium.

This cloud is coming from the direction of the constellation Centaurus. This is the brain child of Paresce and Bowyer of the Space Telescope Science Institute in Baltimore. The scientists believe the galactic cloud will result in a cooling effect here on Earth.

The astrophysicist Piers Corbyn has studied the influence of solar activity on our weather patterns here in the U.K. He is convinced that his research on sunspots can predict the weather with reasonable accuracy. Piers is also open minded to the electric theory of the sun and is cynical about manmade global warming. Piers Corbyn is a London based meteorologist and astrophysicist who believes that the Sun is the primary influence on our weather and climate.

Piers forecasts weather patterns using correlations between sunspots, space weather and the climate. Interestingly Piers Corbyn is also leaning more towards a global cooling forecast for our planet.

This certainly makes sense as the solar data from Ulysses shows a decline in solar wind. A Whitehouse space program adviser believes that the Sun has cooling cycles. John Casey has worked for NASA on the space shuttle programme and he believes that our planet Earth is in a precarious goldilocks zone as far as solar radiation input is concerned.

The Earth's climate in the Northern Hemisphere can easily be disrupted as there is a very narrow margin of error keeping us warm. The space scientist is concerned that the coming decades may become colder due to the Sun going cold. This could lead to food shortages and crop failures in the Northern Hemisphere.

John L. Casey is convinced that the Sun is about to enter a cooling phase soon and has written the books "Cold Sun" and "Dark Winter". Worryingly the space scientist suspects a link between low solar activity and geophysical events such as volcanic eruption and earthquakes.

Other scientists have also published papers suggesting a link between low solar activity and geophysical upheavals here on Earth. Certainly there is a feedback loop between volcanic eruptions and cooler temperatures. The suspended aerosols from volcanic ash can diminish sunlight for years.

Astrophysicist Dr. H. Abdussamatov is the head of space research at the Russian Academy of Science's Pulkovo Observatory in St. Petersburg. He is head of the International Space Station's Astrometria project.

Russian solar physicist Abdussamatov also predicts another ice age within the next thirty years. Dr. Abdussamatov states that we can soon expect the start of the next bicentennial cycle of deep cooling. According to this scientist the solar radiation flux reaching the Earth has decreased since the 1990`s.

This is caused by a decrease of the solar radius and radiative area. In other words he thinks the Sun is shrinking! Abdussamatov feels that the Sun is actually reducing its diameter and says that this will cause a cooling similar to the Maunder Minimum.

Dr. Abdussamatov points out that Earth has experienced such cooling cycles five times over the last 1,000 years. This theory ties in with the solar cooling cycles that Casey talks about in his book "Cold Sun".

Some scientists are giving us a bit more time to prepare for the ice age. The ninety year old distinguished scientist Dr. Fred Singer gave a talk recently about the new ice age. His graphs showed that the major ice age might start within the next two hundred years.

Our great grandchildren may live to see this event and this gives us time to prepare. After our mini ice age ends around the year 2055, Singer thinks the temperatures might possibly climb again, only to fall off dramatically as the ice age commences.

There is no doubt that our major ice age is lurking just around the corner. One day our descendants may even wake up to see that a land bridge has opened up once more between Great Britain and France!

The idea of being able to walk across to France may seem appealing. However one dare not imagine the cataclysmic event that would result in the lowering of the Channel waters to form this land bridge.

The Sun was formed five billion years ago and has circulated around the Galaxy ever since. The Sun has crossed one of the spiral arms called the Orion arm 50 times. A million years ago the Sun entered a dark lane situated on the edge of a spiral arm.

When it exited the dusty arm, the ice age came to an end. This implies that the space dust is facilitating the ice ages. Every time the solar system passes through this dense dusty part of the Galaxy the volume of dust between the Sun and our Earth is denser.

Certainly there is ample evidence that other forms of dust cool Earth`s temperatures. We are definitely at the stage of the arrival of a new ice age and perhaps the space dust theory proposed by Richard Muller helps to explain the onset of our now overdue ice age.

The idea that cosmic dust might periodically cause the planet to cool was first suggested by Richard Muller of the University of California at Berkeley and Gordon MacDonald of the University of California, San Diego, in a short article published in Nature.

Kenneth Farley and Desmond Patterson of the California Institute of Technology in Pasadena have found that the amount of cosmic dust arriving at the seafloor also varies on a 100, 000-year cycle. This intriguing finding exactly mirrors the 100, 000 year cycle of ice ages and interglacials.

Farley discovered that the influx of cosmic dust increased suddenly a million years ago roughly the time when the recent wave of ice ages began. It is possible that a bolide collision in the asteroid belt created a large dust cloud, which somehow triggered the first ice age.

It is scientifically accepted that here on planet Earth **volcanic ash cools the skies. Sulphur aerosol pollution from volcanoes leads to global dimming and a drop in temperatures. This topic of the global cooling effect of volcanic eruptions will now be explored.**

Chapter Two: Volcanic Armageddon.

If a supervolcano erupted today it would unleash a global climatic Armageddon. In the past such eruptions may have resulted in mass extinctions here on Earth. If a large supervolcano such as Yellowstone were to erupt it would unleash a nuclear volcanic winter effect with the dust blocking out the sun for decades. A new ice would arrive within years.

There is also the possibility that our declining magnetic field will facilitate the eruption of our supervolcanoes. Oceanographers have found evidence in deep sea cores that during past magnetic reversals there was a massive increase in volcanic activity. A paper was published in 1970 by Nature magazine by oceanographers J. P. Kennet and N. D. Watkins.

The oceanographers' research showed a mass extinction occurred in the south Pacific which also coincided with a magnetic reversal and ferocious volcanic activity. So just as the magnetic poles were shifting the volcanoes went beserk! Indeed it is thought that Yellowstone last erupted during a magnetic reversal.

Therefore we should be keeping a very close eye on our magnetic field which is declining and shifting rapidly. This could be the silent smoking gun that triggers the overdue eruption at Yellowstone.

A supervolcano is defined as having the capacity to produce a super-eruption that ejects at least 1000 cubic kilometers of volcanic material. **As well as the climatic effects there is danger** from the molten lava and ash. The residents of Pompeii were killed and mummified by waves of fast-moving hot ash and volcanic gasses when Mount Vesuvius erupted in 79AD.

The last known supervolcanic eruption was believed to have occurred about 74,000 years ago at the site today of Lake Toba in Sumatra, Indonesia. It caused a volcanic winter that blocked out the sun for between six to eight years, and resulted in a period of global cooling lasting a thousand years. **Toba is a 1,080-square-mile caldera supervolcano in North Sumatra, Indonesia and it is the only supervolcano in existence that can compare with the size of Yellowstone.**

When Toba erupted it ejected several thousand times more material than erupted from Mount St. Helens in 1980. Some researchers think that Toba's ancient super eruption and the global cold spell it triggered might explain a mystery in the human genome.

Our genes suggest we all come from a lineage of a few thousand people just tens of thousands of years ago. This theory could be true if only a few small groups of humans survived the freezing hostile cold years following the Toba eruption.

There are at least seven supervolcanoes that threaten the future of humanity, including Yellowstone in Yellowstone Wyoming National Park. If Yellowstone erupted 87, 000 people would be killed immediately. On February 19 2018

Yellowstone was hit by ten small earthquakes in one day!

of the mini quakes were by Maple Creek. Seismologists said that the site is under severe strain. A swarm of quakes have been recorded on the Western side of the National park. If Yellowstone blows two thirds of America will be uninhabitable and the ash could precipitate the ice age by blocking out sunlight. Still sure you want to plan a sightseeing trip to this stunning National Park?

Valles Calder is another supervolcano lurking beneath a 175-square-mile Caldera in the middle of northern New Mexico. It last exploded 1.2 million and 1.6 million years ago, blasting ash as far away as Iowa.

As with other calderas, there are still signs of heat below. Hot springs are still active around Valles. Geologists think Valles caldera is caused by the United States' portion of the North American tectonic plate is being pulled apart.

One of the most fearsome calderas in the world is the 150-square-mile Aira caldera in southern Japan. This supervolcano caldera is by the city of Kagoshima. 22,000 years ago 14 cubic miles of material burped out of the ground and formed the Aira caldera, which is now largely Kagoshima Bay. That is equal to about 50 Mount St. Helens eruptions. The Sakura-Jima volcano has been active on and off for the past century and still causes earthquakes today, indicating that the caldera itself is far from sleeping.

Other danger volcanoes waiting to blow are Mount Fuji and Mount Unzen in Japan. In Columbia there is the Nevado del Ruiz, and the Mauna Loa in Hawaii. Iceland of course has many active volcanoes. Let us not forget either that more volcanoes are found beneath the oceans than above.

The supervolcano Uturuncu in Bolivia has been swelling since 1992 and may be preparing to blow. New Zealand is home to the Taupo supervolcano. This scenic visitor attraction is far from dormant and the bubbling hot springs are showing increased vigour.

The Long Valley caldera in California has also been rsiing in the recent decades. This supervolcano erupted 760, 000 years ago and could also be due for a big one. In 1980 there was a

10-inch rise of about 100 square miles of caldera floor.

In the early 1990s, large amounts of carbon dioxide gas from magma below began seeping up through the ground. The gases killed trees in the Mammoth Mountain region of the caldera. When these sorts of signs are present, it could mean an eruption is on the way, say volcanologists.

One of the potentially most dangerous eruptions is that of the Cumbre Vieja in the Canary Islands in Spain. The Cumbre Vieja is an active volcanic ridge on the volcanic island of La Palma. If Cumbre Vieja blows it will collapse into the sea causing massive waves and tsunamis. Such a massive volume of debris would displace the water leading to an instant tidal wave. These tsunamis would race across the seas flooding the west coast of Cornwall and Wales. The computer simulations also predict that tsunamis 80 feet high would surge into the East Coast of America!

The gigantic tidal waves would race across the Atlantic Ocean and drown New York City and other cities all along the East Coast. There would be no warning either and no time to evacuate! The 500 feet high tsunamis would arrive in waves and at terrible speeds!

The imminent collapse of the Cumbre Vieja is a ticking time bomb that is recklessly being ignored by the British and the American governments. There are many signs that the Cumbre Vieja is chronically unstable and many scientists believe it is about to fail and disintegrate into the sea (Day et al 1999).

Recently in October 2017 a wave of low magnitude earthquakes were detected by seismologists coming from the west flank of La Cumbre Vieja. This might be the precursory activity that is warning us that the sleeping giant is getting ready to blow!

There is no doubt that both England and America are in the firing line for a wave of devastating mega tsunamis if this volcano blows itself apart. It is very worrying that volcanic activity is predicted to increase as our magnetic field continues to weaken.

As well as the loss of life from a gigantic tsunami there is a wide body of literature showing the link between volcanic eruptions and cooler temperatures. The sulphur aerosols from volcanic eruptions hang in the skies for a few years like a veil. These aerosols reflect sunlight back into space causing a dimming effect. Even though volcanic eruptions contain greenhouse gases such carbon dioxide the net effect is one of cooling. This cooling effect lasts until the aerosols eventually fall down to Earth as acid rain.

Sulphur dioxide combines with water to form an acid rain. Sulphur dioxide gets converted into sulphuric acid, which then forms aerosols high up in the atmosphere that also serve to block incoming solar radiation for several years after the eruption.

Acid rain is harmful to trees and plant life. There have been numerous eruptions in the twentieth century that have had an impact on incoming solar radiation. These include the volcanic eruption of Mount St Helens in 2008. It produced a dimming plume of ash 14,500 metres high into the atmosphere.

Eyjafjallajökull is a volcano on the Eastern Volcanic Zone in southern Iceland that began to erupt on 14 April 2010. A plume of volcanic ash was ejected several kilometres into the atmosphere potentially causing a hazard for aeroplanes. UK airspace was closed causing significant disruption to travellers.

The engines of planes can become dangerously clogged with ash from volcanic eruptions and cease to function. The disruption to air travel continued when increased explosive activity at the volcano coincided with northerly to north-westerly winds that brought the ash towards Europe.

The volcanic eruption of Mount Tambora, Indonesia, in 1815 was the largest ever recorded and the resulting ash cloud in 1816 gave rise to what is known as "the year without a summer". Fortunately, modern aircraft did not exist back then, as the disruption would have been unimaginable.

Were such a huge eruption to occur today, our modern aviation system would probably be put out of action for months or longer.

The ash plume contains large amounts of microscopic particles of volcanic rock, which can clog up aeroplane engines. Volcanic ash clouds are made up of small abrasive particles that can clog up jet engines that can stop them working. Planes are either re-routed or grounded when there's a danger of flying into ash clouds to ensure the safety of passengers and avoid very costly damage according to Dr David Kerridge, who is the head of Earth Hazards in Edinburgh.

  The year 1816 had diabolical temperatures and snow fell in June. It rained constantly and lack of sunlight throughout the Northern hemisphere. Crops failed and many countries endured famine, poverty and sickness.

  Mount Tambora unleashed an eruption worse than Krakatoa, Washington's Mount Saint Helens, and even Pompeii's Vesuvius. Tambora registered a VEI-7 on the Volcanic Explosivity Index, a metric that measures the size of volcanic eruptions on a scale from VEI-0 (non-explosive) to VEI-8 (megacolossal).

Krakatoa measured a VEI-6, while Mount St. Helens and Vesuvius both rated a VEI-5. When neighbouring volcano Krakatoa erupted in 1883, a huge bang was heard all the way across the Channel in England. French astronomers from Montpelier observed a twenty per cent decrease in solar radiation as ash hung in the skies for three consecutive years. Krakatoa poured 50 million metric tonnes of ash into the skies creating clouds of vitriol.

Giant waves reached heights of 40 m above sea level, hurling ashore coral blocks weighing as much as 600 tons. At least 36,000 people were killed, by the giant sea waves, and 165 coastal villages were destroyed. When the eruption ended, only a third of Krakatoa, remained above sea level. New islands of steaming pumice and ash lay where the sea had once been.

When Tambora erupted in 1815, North American residents reported heavy snow falling as late as the middle of June in 1816. This was the famous American year without a summer. If we were to experience an eruption like Tambora in modern times, the results would be catastrophic. The global population has dramatically risen by billions of people over the past 200 years.

The consequences of a super eruption occurring in modern times would be devastating. Activities like air travel would grind to a halt as volcanic ash can seize up jet engines and cause planes to crash. The global climate change would result in outbreaks of famine and disease.

Experts warn of 90,000 immediate deaths and a 'nuclear winter' across the US if Yellowstone supervolcano erupts. It could release a thick layer of molten ash 1,000 miles away from the National Park. It would be 1,000 times as powerful as the 1980 Mount St Helens eruption'. A haze would hover over the United States, causing temperatures to drop. A supervolcano in the heart of America's northwest has the potential to blanket the continent in ash and create a nuclear winter. A Yellowstone eruption would be one thousand times as powerful as the 1980 Mount St Helens eruption!

Scientists say that we cannot rule out the possibility that an eruption may soon take place. The fact that a major ice age is now due may even coincide with this volcanic eruption.

When Yellowstone in Wyoming last erupted it threw more than 1,000 cubic kilometres of ash and lava into the atmosphere. This is 100 times more than the Mount Pinatubo eruption in the Philippines in 1982, which caused a noticeable period of global cooling.

Professor Bill Mc Guire is an expert on natural hazards. He speculates in his books on natural disasters that this volcano may not be dormant and therefore could erupt at any time in the near future.

The British Professor of geophysical and climate hazards at UCL is convinced that Yellowstone is now due to erupt. He even thinks that an eruption is quite likely to happen soon according to past records! Mc Guire does not agree with other vulcanologists that the caldera is dormant either.

Three super-eruptions at Yellowstone appear to have occurred on a 600,000-700,000 year cycle starting 2.1 million years ago. The most recent took place 640,000 years ago and this data suggesting Yellowstone is overdue for an eruption according to Bill Mc Guire. Worryingly some scientists speculate that low solar activity may also trigger an increase in seismic activity and volcanism and there are recent measured signs of a decrease in solar winds. Could a super eruption be the final catalyst for our descent into our massive ice age lasting 100, 000 years?

There is no doubt that a massive eruption would plunge us into an instant ice age as the ash laden skies become dim and dust particles block out the sunlight. The British climatologist Hubert Lamb was the first scientist to develop a Dust Veil Index to measure the cooling effects of atmospheric dust. Lamb studied the effect of volcanic dust on the Earth`s energy balance.

This dust index was first developed in the year 1970 to quantify the exact effect of volcanic eruptions on our climate. Later this seminal Dust Veil Index was replaced by the Volcanic Explosivity Index that measured the power of eruptions and consequent effects on the climate.

Our return to a grand ice age is now due. The Earth`s axial tilt has decreased which means it receives less solar radiation. Not all geologists are very impressed with the orbital theory of ice ages however.

Some scientists feel that aerial dust might be the missing factor that is involved with initiating ice ages. Dust in the atmosphere also stunts tree growth. This results in narrower tree rings for the years of high dust that is caused by volcanism. The width of tree rings can tell us a lot about the climate for those years of ring growth.

The science of dendrochronology shows how volcanic dust both cools and inhibits plant life. There has to be another causal factor for the overdue major ice age apart from the minor seasonal insolation variables induced by Milankovitch cycles.

There can be no doubt that many volcanoes simultaneously erupting would lead to a global cooling event. An ice age climatic tipping point could well be a major volcanic eruption such as that of Yellowstone. This eruption might even be triggered by a pole shift since magnetic reversals are thought to encourage seismic activity.

The ever bubbling Grand Prismatic hot spring attraction in Yellowstone National Park is among the park's many active hydrothermal features created by the supervolcano. The volcano at Yellowstone National Park in Wyoming and Montana sits atop a huge reserve of molten rock.

The walls of the Grand Canyon of Yellowstone are made from lava and rocks from a supereruption some 630,000 years ago. There are signs that the volcanic underground activity is increasing towards the State of Idaho and therefore Idaho could be site of the next major eruption! The resultant ash cloud would dim the sun for years and even affect the United Kingdom.

If Yellowstone blew then most of the Northern Hemisphere would be plunged into a catastrophic ice age and crops would fail. An eruption of such a powerful supervolcano would plunge the planet into an ice age. A major volcanic eruption could be this secret smoking gun though some experts say that there is only a one in 700,000 annual chance of a volcanic eruption at the site. Let us hope that this optimistic prediction is correct!

Recently the physicist Michio Kaku announced that the ground has risen by ten inches near the caldera. He suspects that the volcano may erupt soon since it may erupt on a 630,000 year cycle that is now due.

During the last 50 years the caldera has been rising at rates comparable to other active and dangerous volcanoes. There may be a link between volcanic eruption and a magnetic reversal. Major volcanism occurred at the Delta Magnetic reversal event 630, 000 years ago around the same time that Yellowstone erupted (Champion 1988).

Yellowstone Volcano's next super eruption will spew vast quantities of gas such as sulphur dioxide, which forms a sulphur aerosol that absorbs sunlight and reflects it back into space. The resulting climate cooling could last up to a decade. The temporary climate shift could alter rainfall patterns.

Severe frosts would cause widespread crop losses leading to famine. But a Yellowstone mega blast would not wipe out life on Earth. There were no mass extinctions after the last three enormous eruptions, nor have other super eruptions triggered total wipeout extinctions in the last few million years.

Recently here have been strange sightings of alien lights and supposed UFO`s hovering above Yellowstone. Earthquake lights are known to appear at times of tectonic stress. Hovering globes of light have been seen before major earthquakes. Eye witnesses have reported several hovering glowing orbs that resemble extraterrestrial space ships! There are now many sightings of these strange UFO like lights hovering!

When nature stresses certain rocks, electric charges are activated, as if a battery is turned on in the Earth's crust. The charges can combine and form a kind of plasma-like state, which can travel at very high velocities and burst out at the surface to make electric discharges in the air. Those discharges make the magical alien UFO light shows. These lights may be a sign that the volcano is getting ready to blow says Brian Clark Howard (National Geographic 2014).

Are we all going to die if Yellowstone erupts? Almost certainly the answer is no said the optimistic Jamie Farrell, a Yellowstone expert and assistant research professor at the University of Utah. There have been quite a few super eruptions in the past couple million years, and we are still around he says! However, scientists agree there is still much to learn about the global effects of super eruptions. The problem with the research is that these massive outbursts are rare. It seems very likely that if a super volcano such as Yellowstone were to erupt, it could help to trigger an instant ice age.

Within days, a fine dusting of ash could fall across Europe, according to a UK Met Office computer forecast commissioned by the BBC. The computer model predicts how ash would spread following a nine-day June eruption of 1000 cubic km of ash and gas from Yellowstone. The model shows that the fallout from a

Yellowstone super-eruption could affect three quarters of the United States.

The greatest danger would be within 1,000 km of the blast where 90 per cent of people could be killed. Large numbers of people would die from suffocation across the country as inhaled ash forms a cement-like mixture in human lungs. The worst of these health effects would not be experienced in Europe where the ash covering would only amount to a dusting. However the ash would dim sunlight globally.

Many people think that lava flows are the most dangerous volcanic hazards, but ash is often the biggest killer. The sulphur particles would combine with water to form acid rain that is deadly to crops and plants.

Because supervolcanoes are highly explosive, much of the magma doesn't get a chance to become lava. Instead it is blasted into countless airborne tiny scorching particles of jagged rock and ash. These razor sharp particles would cut the lungs to ribbons leading to agonising deaths in Wyoming and Idaho.

The most wide reaching effect of a Yellowstone eruption would be colder weather around the globe. Volcanoes inject sulphur gas into the upper atmosphere, forming sulphuric acid aerosols that rapidly spread around the globe. Sulphuric aerosols are the main cause of climatic cooling after an eruption.

Aerosols in the upper atmosphere would also scatter sunlight making the sky look like a cloudy winter morning all day long. The overcast effect would be akin to a nuclear winter. The skies in Europe would appear red in the days after the eruption.

To predict how the climate may be affected, the experts relied on historic data from the Toba supervolcano in Indonesia about 74,000 years ago and computer model forecasts commissioned from the UK Met Office and the Max Planck Institute in Hamburg.

Experts believe a Yellowstone eruption would inject 2,000 million tonnes of sulphur above the Earth's surface. Once there it would take three weeks for the resulting sulphuric acid aerosols to cloak the globe with devastating effects. Global annual average temperatures would drop by up to 10 degrees, and the Northern Hemisphere could cool by up to 12 degrees!

Some geophysicists are convinced that there is a correlation between increased volcanic activity and declining magnetic field strength. Volcanic eruptions also correlate well with a full magnetic field reversal. Major volcanic eruptions took place at the Jaramillo magnetic reversal and at the Brunhes - Matuyama magnetic reversal around 780, 000 years ago (Schnepp and Hradeztky 1994).

It is possible that major volcanic super eruptions might occur as our magnetic field is plummeting and this will bring on an instant ice age. Increased seismic activity could even affect the precarious San Andreas Fault affecting the densely populated California.

The Earth`s magnetic field is presently decreasing at an unprecedented rate and the South Atlantic anomaly is still growing. The European Space Agency ESA reported in 2014 that the magnetic field is now declining ten times faster than previously thought and could be preparing to flip. Magnetic North is now slowly drifting towards Siberia.

If the magnetic field collapses it would wreak havoc on our satellites and power grids. If a large solar storm arrived it could knock out our electricity supplies leaving us at the mercy of an ice age. Likewise the radiation from galactic cosmic rays that seed clouds would be dangerously increased without a magnetic shield .This increased cloud cover would also facilitate an ice age. We should take the link between declining magnetic field strength and volcanism seriously.

The medieval cold weather of the Dark Ages in Great Britain could have been exacerbated by massive volcanic eruptions. Scientists suggest that the 500 year long icy cold period in the Dark Ages was triggered by an unusual episode of four massive volcanic eruptions. This caused the actual skies to appear darker than normal due to ash and hence the term Dark Ages was coined. This increased volcanism coincided with a weakening of Atlantic currents that caused the cool period to persist for centuries (Miller et al 2012).

The study, led by the University of Colorado Boulder and the National Center for Atmospheric Research suggest that an unusual, 50 year episode of four massive volcanic eruptions triggered the Little Ice Age between 1275 and 1300.

The Black Death plague of 1349 then wreaked havoc on a population weakened by the preceding years of cold weather. The medieval cold weather caused crop failure and famine. The weakened population was soon ravaged by a terrible plague. People dropped dead like flies in the streets of London and around half of the population died from bubonic plague.

The cold summers following the medieval eruptions caused an expansion of sea ice and a related weakening of Atlantic currents. According to computer simulations by the University of Colorado Boulder, the ocean currents slowed. This slowing of currents would also have caused a decrease in the flow of the warming Gulf Stream.

The study used analysis of ice and sediment data, with powerful computer climate models and provides new evidence in a longstanding scientific debate over the cause of the medieval Little Ice Age. The Little Ice Age in the Dark Ages was caused by decreased summer solar radiation, and several erupting volcanoes that cooled the planet by ejecting sulphate aerosol particles. These particles reflected sunlight back into space.

"This is the first time anyone has clearly identified the specific onset of the cold times marking the start of the Little Ice Age," says lead author Gifford Miller of the University of Colorado Boulder.

"We also have provided an understandable climate feedback system that explains how this cold period could be sustained for a long period of time. If the climate system is hit again and again by cold conditions from volcanic eruptions there appears to be a cumulative cooling effect."

"Our simulations showed that the volcanic eruptions had a profound cooling effect," says scientist Bette Otto-Bliesner, a co-author of the study. The eruptions could have triggered a chain reaction, affecting sea ice and ocean currents in a way that lowered temperatures for centuries (Miller 2012).

It is interesting to note that the Atlantic Meridional Overturning Circulation (AMOC) was thought to have been affected during this cold volcanically active spell. It shows how the feedback loops such as increasing volcanism act synergistically with the seas to further bring down temperatures. This circulating ocean conveyor incorporating the Gulf Stream is vital in bringing warmth to our shores. The Gulf Stream and its impact on our climate will now be discussed.

Chapter 3: Gulf Stream Alert

London is a dynamic hub of commerce and a thriving city of global importance. London is also one of the wealthiest cities in the entire world. Finally London is also is closer to the North Pole than Newfoundland, where temperatures **seldom get above zero in January and February. It is tempting to speculate that perhaps one of the reasons that Great Britain is so wealthy and successful may in part be due to its temperate climate.**

Could our economic position be placed in peril by a plummeting climate? If Britain is plunged into an ice age will its economy experience a similar fall? London is a vast dynamic hub of business and finance.

Could this prosperity decline if our capital city becomes covered in snow drifts as happened in recent harsh winters? When large amounts of snow arrive in our country everything grinds to a halt.

The British Isles are bathed in the balmy waters and air streams gifted to our shores by the Gulf Stream. We tend therefore to forget just how far north we actually are.

We are on the same latitudes as freezing snow covered towns in Canada. Yet we remain relatively frost free and frequently enjoy some mild winters. This is mostly thanks to warm westerlies and warm currents from the Gulf Stream.

When our winters become harsh and bitterly cold it is often the result of Northern polar air masses or cold east winds from Siberia, colloquially known as the "Beast from the East".

Our mild climate owes a debt of gratitude to the beneficent Gulf Stream. The entire East Coast of America from Florida to Newfoundland also benefits from these warm waters. The Gulf Stream enables the waters of Florida to remain balmy and warm during winter months. There can be no doubt that the American economy also benefits from the warmth gifted by the Gulf Stream.

A Horizon documentary was recently made about the weakening of our Gulf Stream. The programme was called "Britain the new Alaska". The premise of the documentary is that fresh non salty ice melt water is leading to a shutdown of our Gulf Stream.

So a global warming may lead to a cooling in Great Britain. It seems that the feedback loops are mostly weighted towards an ice age for Great Britain. Even if it warms elsewhere in the globe, Britain is always in the firing line for an ice age! We cannot escape the ice and snow as all the odds are stacked against us.

This current of water originates in the warm Gulf of Mexico. The Gulf Stream

is a part of the thermohaline circulation of waters sometimes known as AMOC.

The thermo refers to the warmth and the haline refers to the saltiness of the water. The thermohaline circulation is mainly triggered by deep cold water masses in the Atlantic and warm water masses in **the Southern Ocean.**

It is also caused by differences in salinity or the saltiness of the water. These differences propel the waters to travel in a constant loop hence the term Atlantic Meridional Overturning Circulation, (Rahmstorf 2003).

A part of the thermohaline circulation branches off to become the Gulf Stream. The benefits of the Gulf Stream cannot be overestimated. It is said that this warm current brings us the equivalent heat of up to one million power stations.

More conservative estimates put it at around 27000 power stations worth of free heat! Either way a substantial amount of free energy and warmth is brought to our fortunate shores and to Northern Europe. No doubt this extra energy has also helped our economy to prosper.

Recently there have been plans to directly harness this free energy source using underwater turbines off the coast of America. Using the temperature difference between the warm and cold water it may be possible to turn it into hydrothermal power. Certainly there is a lot of potential energy that is waiting to be harvested.

Were the Gulf Stream to slow down completely there would be a substantial heat and energy deficit. Homes would need more heating to compensate for the drop in temperatures. A study published in Nature indicated that the Gulf Stream or North Atlantic conveyor has slowed by 30%.

If it were to fail it could cause another ice age in Northern Europe. This scientific study showed that the Gulf Stream has slowed by 30% since 1957. If it stopped altogether temperatures would fall dramatically in the countries warmed by it (Bryden et al 2005).

This deficit would have to be made up for by increasing our energy supplies. Instead of preserving our vital energy infrastructure we are embarking on a path of power station closure in Great Britain. This may turn out to be the worst policy ever implemented by any Government!

During some of the recent unusually freezing cold winters experienced in the U.K. the coal powered Drax power station in Yorkshire was working flat out to keep the lights on as power use surged.

Without this hardworking power station, people would have frozen, and the already high winter mortality rate would have risen. Yet our life saving coal power stations are all marked for closure in a policy designed to stave off global warming!

Meanwhile there are worrying signs that the rate of flow of our Gulf Stream may be decreasing. Bill Turrell is an oceanic scientist from the Marine Laboratory in Aberdeen.

The team is based in the Faroe Islands off Scotland. Turrell has found a significant drop in the level of saltiness in the water off the coast of Scotland. His team were very surprised at the steep decline in salinity and the graphs showed a precipitous decline in saltiness of the water.

This drop in salinity could lead to a slowing down of the AMOC. There is evidence that the current has slowed due to fresh meltwater entering the thermohaline circulation. This fresh glacial meltwater is diluting the saltiness. This dilution caused by cold fresh water then weakens the current.

This dilution then slows the Gulf Stream until it eventually stops altogether.

Scientists now believe that we are getting dangerously close to this cut off point. The unvoiced question is whether the AMOC (Atlantic Meridional Overturning Circulation) currently known to be in decline, could drop off suddenly.

This event was depicted in the film "The Day After Tomorrow". This scenario would cause temperatures to plummet. Computer models and evidence collated by Stefan Rahmstorf of the Potsdam Institute for Climate Impact Research in Germany suggests that global warming could turn off the North Atlantic Drift, causing temperatures in northwest Europe to drop by 5 °C or more.

Bill Turrell has found evidence that fits in with Rahmstorf's predictions.

He analysed more than 17 000 measurements of seawater salinity between Shetland and the Faroe Islands since 1893. Turrell found that in each of the past two decades the salinity of the deep water flowing south has dropped by 0.01 grams of salt per kilogram of seawater. So its density has probably also decreased by 0.01 kilograms per cubic metre per decade.

"This is the largest change we have seen in the outflow in the last 100 years," says Turrell. "It is consistent with models showing the stopping of the pump and the conveyor belt."

In the 1950s the salinity of the outflow was so stable it was used to calibrate equipment; but now things are changing.

Bill Turrell said that this was the most dramatic data he had seen in his entire career. This data has been confirmed by data sets taken by other researchers. However there is some speculation that this measured drop in speed and salinity may be a periodical and cyclical process and that the circulation may recover again (Jackson, et al 2016).

Danssgaard Oeschger Events are recorded temperature changes in the thermohaline circulation (Dansgaard et al 1993). These are dramatic ocean temperature swings that have been recorded in ice core samples.

The reader may recall that the graphs show a rapid decline into the start of the ice age and then later the graph shows rises of temperature in the ice age itself. These swings in the Atlantic Ocean temperature became known as Dansgaard-Oeschger events. These are abbreviated to D-O events for simplicity.

These events take place roughly every 1470 years. It seems that the melting ice caps and freshwater from glaciers disrupts the thermohaline circulation. This freshwater reduces the salinity and so slows down the thermohaline circulation.

This leads to cooler temperatures in the North. However the Southern Hemisphere may not be affected as it is a bipolar effect. It seems that when the Northern Hemisphere warms up, the ice melts and the AMOC slows down. This in turn cools the land masses such as Great Britain. Therefore these D-O events will likely cool Great Britain.

There is speculation as to what causes this ice to melt and the Sun is one factor. Even during previous freezing ice ages there is evidence that now and then the Sun woke up so to speak and warmed up. The periodic nature of our Sun was discussed in the previous chapter.

The awakening of our Sun could have resulted in ice caps and glaciers melting and more freshwater being released in the oceans. This is known as a Dansgaard-Oeschger event. These D-O warming and cooling events have been occurring during our present interglacial the Holocene as well as during the ice ages (Bond et al 2001).

A paleoclimatologist called Hartmut Heinrich discovered that marine sediments provide evidence of large swings in ocean temperatures. Large rises and falls in temperature have been deduced from marine sediments. These sediments provide evidence that cyclical climatic processes are taking place in the Atlantic Ocean currents.

It is likely that these changes in Ocean temperature are induced by solar cycles. There are periodic falls and rises in the North Atlantic temperature throughout the last ice age (Elliot et al 2002). This phenomenon may also occur during an interglacial. Evidence of eight D-O events has been found from ice core sampling as well as marine sediments (EPICA 2004).

The last ice age was characterized by rapid and hemispherically asynchronous climate oscillations, whose origin remains unresolved. Ice cores from Greenland and Antarctica show that sudden temperature shifts, occurred every 1500 years.

They were also out of synch in the two hemispheres. When it got cold in the north, it grew warm in the south, and vice versa. Scientists have implicated the culprit behind these bipolar seesaws as the AMOC.

This ocean circulation in turn was most likely influenced by our Sun which may periodically wake up or become sleepy to put it in metaphorical terms. There can be no doubt that the Atlantic Ocean plays a central role in abrupt climate change (Hand; Henry et al 2016).

The AMOC brings warm surface waters north and send cold, deeper waters south. In a matter of decades, temperatures plummeted in the north, as the currents brought less warmth in that direction. Meanwhile, the backlog of warm, southern waters allowed the Southern Hemisphere to heat up.

Heinrich Events:

Heinrich events are a more dramatic and deadlier version of the Dansgaard-Oeschger events. A Heinrich event is a rapid release of huge amounts of icebergs from the Canadian ice sheet. An iceberg armada Heinrich event once discharged as much ice into the Atlantic Ocean as the entire ice cap of Greenland.

This Heinrich event raised ancient sea levels by ten meters. The icy water brought incredible amounts of freshwater to the North Atlantic. Because freshwater is less dense than saltwater, it can stall the AMOC, preventing the ocean circulation's engine. This is because the circulation depends on a difference between salt and fresh water to keep moving and turning.

The climatologist James Hansen has written a scary book about Heinrich events called "Storms of my Grandchildren". Hansen writes that man could warm the planet with anthropogenic emissions and cause a catastrophic ice melting Heinrich event. Certainly this a riveting book and thought provoking book.

There is no doubt that Heinrich ice melting events could be deadly. As I watched a nuclear missile test in North Korea, the thought crossed my mind that a nuclear blast shock wave might one day cause a major ice melting Heinrich event.

Younger Dryas:

The Younger Dryas ice age event occurred around 12,900 to 11,700 years ago. The Northern Hemisphere fell into a deep chill. The sharp drop in temperature of the Younger Dryas was relatively sudden, and took place in decades. This resulted in a temperature decline of up to 6 degrees Celsius.

A drop of only 5 degrees Celsius is enough to precipitate an ice age in the Northern Hemisphere. There was colder weather over much of the temperate Northern Hemisphere during the Younger Dryas.

There is evidence of a major extinction event at the Younger Dryas event 12, 900 years ago as the ice age was coming to an end.

The giant ice age mammals such as the giant sloth, sabre tooth tiger and the giant short faced bear died out overnight. Mammoths have been found with food still in their mouths as though they suddenly died. Perhaps the extinction was caused by a comet or perhaps a supervolcano erupted.

This cataclysmic event resulted in the ice age resuming with ferocity even though it was due to end. An eruption or asteroid impact set off the Younger Dryas cool period in the Northern Hemisphere that lasted for 1300 years before the ice age finally ended. It was named the Younger Dryas due to an abundance of alpine flower pollen found (Biello 2009).

The Younger Dryas mini ice age event is thought to have been aided by a decline in the strength of the AMOC which transports warm water from the equator towards the North Pole. The slowing of the ocean circulation exacerbated the colder climate. This decline is thought to have been caused by an influx of fresh cold water from North America into the Atlantic.

The Younger Dryas was a period of climatic change, but the effects were complex and variable. In the Southern Hemisphere, there was a slight warming as this is a bipolar seesaw effect (Carlson 2013). The Younger Dryas data suggest that we need to keep a close eye on our ocean circulation patterns since the temperature dropped dramatically in a very short time when the current changed. Indeed the transition from the greenhouse to the icehouse was probably like a madhouse!

Professor Wallace Broecker described the Gulf Stream as a big heat machine that could prove to be the Achilles heel of our climate if it slowed.

Broecker wrote a book called "Unpleasant surprises in the greenhouse?" in 1987. Without our Gulf Stream we would perhaps lose the equivalent of one million power stations` worth of heat.

Even if the amount of heat lost was less than this estimate it would still make a substantial difference to the climate of Great Britain. However not all scientists are in complete agreement as to how much heat exactly the Gulf stream brings to our shores and this is an area of scientific debate.

The data from previous glacials shows the Atlantic Ocean currents exert a powerful effect on our climate.

Wallace Broecker has spent his entire life studying the Gulf Stream and he believes that it is vital for our climate to stay warm.

The Gulf Stream also brings a great deal of warmth to the East coast of America. There is no doubt that ice sheets are melting since the waters of the Gulf Stream is becoming less saline. **The AMOC transports a large amount of heat into the North Atlantic where it is given up to the atmosphere and helps regulate the climate in Europe and North America.**

This could be a warning sign of an imminent ice age. If Greenland continues to lose ice it can make the AMOC less saline and this in turn can cool down Northern Hemisphere land masses. It is shown that in the past huge injections of freshwater can falter the finely tuned overturning circulation of the ocean currents.

The fresh water then disrupts the salinity of the water which makes the circulation less efficient. It seems to a case of heads you win heads you lose as the odds always seem to favour an ice age.

The major effect of a slowing AMOC is expected to be cooler winters and summers around the North Atlantic. A study, published in the current issue of the *Quarterly Journal of the Royal Meteorological Society*, suggests that the Gulf Stream accounts for around 10 per cent of the winter temperature differences between Britain and Newfoundland, Canada. The scientists found that the reason for Britain's mild weather was twofold.

First, there is a genuine maritime effect of being surrounded by a relatively warm body of water. Second, this maritime influence is bolstered by south-westerly winds bringing a warm air mass from the south. These winds would not blow if the Rockies did not exist, the researchers found (Seager 2002).

So perhaps Great Britain`s milder climate is being facilitated by the Rocky Mountains. However we should not rest on our laurels and hope that the Rockies will prevent the arrival of our overdue ice age.

The Atlantic Meridional Overturning Circulation and Gulf Stream will also be affected by low solar activity. If the

Atlantic conveyor belt were to shut down even temporarily the land around the North Atlantic would cool down by a massive drop of six degrees Celsius.

This shut down can be caused by increasing fresh meltwater since a saltier current is more vigorous than a less saline circulation. Paradoxically this is one way that a global warming event such as the melting of Greenland`s ice sheets could result in a cooling for the Northern hemisphere.

If Greenland ice melts, Great Britain will end up with a cooler climate as a result of this freshwater discharge. Freshwater flux from Greenland is composed of melt runoff from ice discharge and calving icebergs.

The amount of freshwater flux from Greenland was relatively stable from the late 1970's to the mid 1990's, and then began to increase. Increased freshwater flux could weaken the Atlantic Meridional Overturning Circulation (Yang et al 2016).

The Cryosat-2 Satellite measures the thickness of Arctic sea ice. However it has been found that the measurements can be out by as much as 25 per cent due to snow salinity. Everyone is concerned about the thinning and loss of Arctic ice.

At the moment there is an advance/retreat pattern of ice formation that is also linked to the seasons. Despite compelling images that Arctic ice is shrinking the most recent data showed that Arctic sea ice increased by 2075 km3 in February 2018. However there is no doubt that Arctic amplification will periodically melt the ice.

So it seems that a warming of the Arctic will ultimately bring cold weather to the British Isles. Every roll of the dice is constantly weighted towards a cold climate for Great Britain!

So we can forget all about the grape vineyards that global warming enthusiasts have promised us here in Old Blighty! The obvious fact is glaring us all in the face. We are living in an ice house not a greenhouse as there is a plentiful accumulation of snow and ice on our planet.

If global warming did take off we would be in a genuine ice free greenhouse once more. There would not be a trace of snow nor ice anywhere in the entire globe if the

Earth was really warming up. Therefore if it snows it is not because of global warming, but because the planet is still in a cooling phase known as an icehouse!

When the recent snowstorms arrived in North America some people blamed the heavy snows on precipitation caused by a global warming of the five Great Lakes. The reason it snows is because it is cold and if the planet was truly warm we would be living in a greenhouse with tropical forests at the Poles. We are living in an icehouse and we can expect a lot more heavy snow in our icy future!

There could be other geological reasons than a presumed anthropogenic warming that may account for the melting Arctic ice. Could one of these causal factors be submarine volcanism? There are over one million volcanoes beneath the sea and hydrothermal vents are found near these underwater volcanoes.

The famous Ring of Fire is 25,000 miles long and consists of more than 450 underwater volcanoes in the Pacific Ocean. Volcanoes at mid ocean ridges account for 75% of the magma on Earth (Speight and Henderson 2010).

Scientists have still not mapped all of the planet`s submarine volcanoes and this especially applies to the Arctic region. In 2011 an undersea volcano erupted off the coast of Oregon that scientists had not known existed. Even the Antarctic is part of the active Ring of Fire with a very active volcano called Mount Erebus.

In fact Mount Erebus is *the* most active volcano in Antarctica. The juxtaposition of a warm ocean caused by subterranean volcanism and cold growing ice sheets produced a monster storms at the start of the last ice age.

The geologist George Kukla thinks that the start of our last ice age, the End-Eemian, was a time of terrible storms over the oceans (New York Times 16 Feb.1999). This theory of warm oceans and cold skies producing monster storms is aptly depicted by the blockbuster film "The Day After Tomorrow

It is theoretically possible that such super snow storms arose in previous ice ages. The transition from the warm Eemian interglacial to the last ice age may have been a time of climatic chaos. If the Arctic waters do warm it will lead to evaporation of moisture into the cold air resulting in massive snow storms.

The North Atlantic Oscillation is a system of air pressure that affects the weather. During the months of November to April, the NAO is responsible for much of the variability of weather in the North Atlantic region, affecting wind speed and wind direction changes, changes in temperature and moisture distribution and the intensity, number and track of storms.

A negative North Atlantic Oscillation strongly correlates with cold U.S. winters.

The NAO was in a very negative phase during the unusually cold snowy winter of 2009/2010. It had not been in such a position since 1865 when records of it began. This rare phenomenon results in a warmer Arctic but colder continents pattern of weather. So one can see that there is a bipolar effect whereby when the Arctic warms, the cold air is often displaced elsewhere (Overland & Wang 2010).

If the Gulf Stream stopped altogether it would lead to an ice age in Great Britain and Northern Europe in less than three years. There is no doubt that the economy would suffer as our infrastructure grinds to a halt.

Think of the chaos in London a few years when unexpected heavy snow disrupted travel and there were desperate cries of "where are the snowploughs?" which almost resulted in a Minister for snowy weather being created!

Parts of North America might also resemble the snowy scenes from the blockbuster film "The Day After Tomorrow" if the Gulf Stream stalls. This film sensationalises the idea of an abrupt climate change. The film shows the sudden shutting down of the thermohaline circulation which forms part of our Gulf Stream.

This part of the film is entirely feasible and studies show that this oceanic circulation event has happened before thousands of years ago. However in the film this shutdown of the thermohaline circulation is caused by manmade global warming and is not a natural cyclical event.

The film depicts massive vortexes of super powerful hurricanes known as hypercanes. The Earth may have experience hypercanes in the distant past. Extreme conditions are needed to cause a hypercane such as a large volcanic eruption or asteroid strike. A huge temperature difference between the ocean and the skies is also needed to form a hypercane.

A hypercane would have a wind speed of over 500mph or 800km per hour and would extend high up into the stratosphere. Hypercanes caused by an impact bollide have occurred on Earth in the ancient past and may have given rise to extinction events (Kerry et al 1995).

Conventional hurricanes do not extend into this higher level of the atmosphere. The stratosphere is a very cold layer of Earth`s atmosphere.

Remember the stratosphere is where the ultra freezing noctilucent polar stratospheric clouds are formed by ice crystals at minus 85 degrees Celsius.

In the film "The Day After Tomorrow" the massive hypercanes that are hundreds of miles wide, create a vortex that sucks down this freezing cold air from the stratosphere.

This leads to an instant ice age in the film. This film is based on a book by Art Bell and Whitley Strieber about a superstorm that is produced by global warming.

However such giant storm cells are unlikely in real life to develop over dry land as they do in the film. Hurricanes usually form over water. However there is no doubt that a hypercane, which is a massive type of hurricane, may have once blown with terrible ferocity over Earth.

An atmospheric scientist from MIT, Dr. Emanuel Kerry, speculates an asteroid impact was able to super heat the oceans. Extreme heating of the oceans would have theoretically been able to give rise to a hypercane.

Such a massive wind force could have flattened the dinosaurs in one fell swoop. The super strong wind would also have stripped the protective ozone layer away leading to a vast influx of deadly radiation hitting the Earth.

Scientists also wonder if a major impact may have caused the end of snowball earth or deep freezes in our distant past by throwing up vast amounts of energy that melted the ice.

There are many underwater sources of geothermal heat that could warm the Arctic and melt ice thereby lead to a displacement of cold water into our Gulf Stream circulation.

For instance there is the underwater Gakkel Ridge. **The Gakkel Ridge is the deepest and most remote portion of the global mid-ocean ridge system. It extends 1,100 miles from north of Greenland to Siberia, beneath the Arctic ice cap.**

The mid ocean ridge is a volcanically active mountain range that runs beneath the North and South Atlantic Oceans, the Arctic Ocean, the Indian Ocean, and the South Pacific.

Underwater hydrothermal vents are seldom included in climate models. However even with a massive heat input from underwater volcanism it is unlikely that a slowing down of the AMOC would lead to the formation of massive hurricanes funnelling air from the stratosphere.

The huge superstorm vortex depicted in this gripping film is also unlikely to form as a result of carbon dioxide induced global warming.

The consequences of the Gulf Stream stalling would still be appalling in ways that we have yet to experience. Professor Wallace Broecker said that the Gulf Stream is the Achilles heel of the ocean conveyor belt circulation.

He is very concerned that East Coast of America would freeze if the Gulf Stream stopped. Scotland benefits greatly from the Gulf Stream which allows the west coast to grow warm weather plants. Scotland is also on the same latitude as Hudson Bay where polar bears are found! If the Gulf Stream continues to lose salinity it could bring a new ice age for Europe and Great Britain.

Our oceans act as huge heat reservoirs and the heat is circulated back into the atmosphere via the hydrosphere. The world`s oceans maintain a thermal balance across the globe.

According to Fred Hoyle it is possible that the thermal equilibrium could collapse within decades and initiate an ice age. If oceans start to lose heat and energy from the weakening sun, the thermal equilibrium can be affected. Ocean currents may be affected by a cooling inertia causing the Gulf Stream to weaken.

If enough water vapour ices up into shiny diamond like ice crystals then further heat is lost and reflected back into space.

Once the ice dust veil is locked into place high in the stratosphere, it becomes self sustaining.

The ice veil attracts more and more freezing nuclei in a chain reaction. The water vapour starts to fall more often as snow instead of rain as heat is lost from a diminished hydrosphere. We will also start to see more noctilucent mother of pearl clouds that are made of fine ice particles.

Chapter 4: Noctilucent Clouds

There are many varieties of clouds such as cirrus, stratus and nimbus. This chapter will discuss a rare shimmering cloud formation called noctilucent clouds. Noctilucent means night shining and these clouds appear to shimmer in the twilight sky. In 2016 the media excitedly reported that astonishingly beautiful and rare cloud formations were being sighted over the north of England and Scotland.

The press reported that strange and beautiful clouds were seen hovering over the cold skies of England. These clouds were a rare phenomenon known as noctilucent clouds. These clouds are stunningly beautiful.

They are also known as nacreous clouds since they shimmer with the opalescent colours that are similar to Mother of pearl. Noctilucent clouds are found high up in the stratosphere in Polar regions and so are also known as Polar Stratospheric Clouds or PSC`s.

These clouds appear to be a recent phenomenon. There was no recorded sighting of these clouds before the year 1885. Satellite data shows that these high altitude frozen clouds have been increasing exponentially during the last few decades.

The Aeronomy of Ice in the Mesosphere, AIM satellite, is dedicated to the study of noctilucent clouds. Intriguingly there has been increased sighting of these clouds in the Northern Hemisphere.

Previously the nacreous cloud formations had only been sighted in Antarctica. The nacreous clouds are also becoming much brighter. The shimmering iridescent clouds are formed at temperatures of minus 85 degrees Celsius. This temperature is colder than average stratospheric temperatures. The implication of this finding is that the upper atmosphere is becoming much colder and it is also shrinking.

These high altitude clouds are comprised of ice particles. Clouds generally don't form in the stratosphere. Typically, it's far too dry there for ice crystals or supercooled water droplets to develop. Therefore the recent appearance of these stratospheric clouds that have been over the North of England and Scotland is something of a rarity. Usually, noctilucent clouds are only seen over the freezing Antarctic.

These clouds are composed of ice crystals and therefore could be a warning that Earth is getting colder. The late Sir Fred Hoyle thought that ice crystals in the upper atmosphere would facilitate an ice age. During winter, when there is little sunlight in the Polar region, the stratospheric polar vortex strengthens and locks out warmer air.

This creates extraordinarily cold temperatures in the stratosphere. Water vapour in the stratosphere then changes to ice crystals.

Nacreous clouds form in the stratosphere, at 70,000 feet. This height is more than twice as high as commercial airliners fly, according to NASA. This is also where the ozone layer resides. It is very dry in the mesosphere layer that is 50 miles up. This makes it all the more difficult for these polar stratospheric clouds to form. Scientists believe that these clouds are involved in reactions that destroy the ozone layer.

Nacreous or polar stratospheric clouds, the rare phenomena adorned the British sky in the wake of Storm Henry in February 2016. Henry battered the northern U.K. with winds up to 60 miles per hour (97 kilometers per hour), causing flooding and caused major power outages.. The cold air the storm blew in also led to the formation of beautiful clouds.

Andrew Klekociuk, an atmospheric scientist said to the National Geographic "These clouds reveal extreme conditions in the atmosphere and promote chemical changes that lead to destruction of vital stratospheric ozone."

Noctilucent Nacreous Clouds

The type of polar stratospheric clouds (PSC`s) that have been appearing over North England are the type 2 PSC`s. These are even colder than type I PSC`s and only ever form in the extreme cold of the Antarctic.

It is very unusual for clouds that form in temperatures of minus 85 degrees Celsius to be observed over the United Kingdom. These super freezing clouds should not be able to form over our clement Island. Noctilucent clouds of this colder type are observed over Antarctica and rarely appear in the Northern hemisphere. Something strange is going on over the skies of Great Britain!

This could be the first important sign that a mini ice age is on its way to Great Britain. The areas of Britain that may be most affected by this coming ice age may be North of Yorkshire which is roughly where the last ice sheets of the major ice age reached.

These clouds destroy ozone and this leads to more cooling, since loss of ozone allows more heat to escape into space. Manmade chemicals such as CFC`s destroy ozone and so it seems that we are contributing to a global cooling with our pollution.

Other "greenhouse" gases such as methane and carbon dioxide also cause stratospheric cooling and encourage the formation of polar stratospheric clouds according to the meteorologist Jeff Masters. So the effect of our much maligned greenhouse gases appears to be one of stratospheric cooling rather than warming!

Perhaps people are right to be concerned about these trace gases as if we are heading for an ice age they can exacerbate the problem. This cooling and thinning of our atmosphere has affected orbiting satellites and caused an increased drag towards Earth.

Many atmospheric scientists tracking satellites are noticing this thinning of the thermosphere such as Robert Kerr, Director of the National Science Foundation Division of Atmospheric Sciences.

Professor Gary E. Thomas of the University of Colorado Boulder is a world expert on these rare shimmering clouds. He agrees that methane and carbon dioxide could become frozen at the mesospheric layer and that these trace gases will enable these clouds to form. He predicts that such clouds will be increasingly seen often over the skies of America.

Professor Thomas is concerned of the effect that industrial emissions may have on our upper atmosphere. It seems that the dice is weighted towards a major cooling event.

The so called greenhouse gases can actually turn into ice crystals and thus act as a cooling feedback. I am starting to think that carbon dioxide is more dangerous in its other less known role as a cooling agent. It is rather ironic that the much feared greenhouse gases may be dangerous icehouse gases instead!

Orbits of satellites are drifting because the ionosphere is becoming 17 degrees Celsius cooler per decade. Our upper atmosphere is also shrinking and is now 3% less dense. Could these be warning signs of our overdue ice age? This theory of mine is given support by the findings of Professor Tom Woods. Professor Woods found a link between a shrinking upper atmosphere and low solar radiation (Woods 2010).

So as the sunspots decrease and our solar wind declines the protective atmosphere shrinks bringing freezing cold outer space ever nearer. As the atmosphere becomes less dense the cosmic rays bombard us, and freezing nacreous cloud formations become more prevalent.

We should take this appearance of these rare clouds very seriously. It is a warning that our upper atmosphere is freezing out and the perils of deep space are drawing ever closer.

With so much focus on the global warming hypothesis we may be in danger of ignoring these warning signs of an imminent cooling.

There is no knowing what the level of severity of the coming ice age will be. There is evidence that our present interglacial the Holocene is somewhat cooler than previous interglacials in our climatological paleohistory. Therefore it is not unreasonable to theorise that the coming ice age may be more severe than previous ice age glacials.

If this is correct then the cold ice sheets may well extend over the whole of Great Britain and Wales. During the last ice age the massive ice sheet stopped just shy of North Oxford. This serendipitous fact will doubtless please the global warming advocate academics in my home city! Perhaps Oxford is the city of global warming after all!

We should however take the warning of a major cooling very seriously. The atmosphere is giving us a stunning visual display that all is not well in the stratospheric air masses over our tiny Island. Since we are now overdue a major ice age glaciation event it would seem reasonable to infer that the new ice age is slowly dawning. Our atmosphere is shrinking because it is cooling rather than warming and solar radiation is declining.

In January 2017 colder type 2 Polar Stratospheric noctilucent clouds were filmed over Finland. It seems that this once rare phenomenon is becoming increasingly more visible. If we ignore this warning sign that our climate is changing to ice age conditions we will be taken by a horrible surprise one day.

There is some evidence that an ice age may not come on gradually over thousands of years. Some studies indicate that an ice age can arrive in a matter of years, weeks or even days.

Ice crystals high up in the atmosphere may also lead to major cooling according to Fred Hoyle's theory of cold ice dust particles leading to ice age conditions (Hoyle, Ice 1979).

The late Sir Fred Hoyle theorised that as long as the water vapour in our atmosphere remained warm enough an ice age could be avoided. However if the water turned to tiny ice crystals the albedo effect would be enormous.

The transport of water vapour must cause a precipitation rate of about 50 cm to keep the water vapour temperature above -50 degrees Celsius to prevent ice crystal formation.

For comparison, the present day world-wide average of the precipitation rate is about 80 cm of rain, sufficient to prevent ice crystal formation, but not by a wide margin.

If the surface layers of the Atlantic Ocean were to cool to the point where an annual average rainfall of 50 cm cannot be maintained, the consequent formation of an atmospheric haze of ice crystals would plunge the Earth immediately back into an instant ice age (Hoyle 1979).

Therefore we need to be vigilant about any increase in icy stratospheric cloud formations as they could be a warning sign that water vapour is icing up into sparkling crystals. Remember that water vapour is the main greenhouse gas in our atmosphere and not carbon dioxide. Water vapour only functions as a greenhouse gas in vapour form.

If it turns to minute ice crystals it becomes a freezing agent instead. The shining ice crystals in turn reflect the sunlight back into deep space. A terrifying albedo effect starts to unfold that is beyond our control.

The diamond dust veil then initiates an ice age. Noctilucent clouds may be stunningly beautiful to look at but they may be the ominous portents of an icy future for Great Britain. We ignore this warning sign at our peril!

Chapter 5: Deadly Cosmic Rays

Cloud cover helps to cool the Earth via the albedo effect. White clouds reflect sunlight back into space in a similar way that ice reflects the sunlight. The albedo effect helps to cool our planet.

Therefore if cloud cover were to increase, the Earth would become cooler. Think of the difference a cloud can make to a nice sunny day. When the clouds arrive the temperature difference can often be felt immediately.

Another way that clouds cool temperature is by locking up water vapour which acts as a greenhouse gas in our atmosphere when it is dissipated. This has a net cooling effect. Joel Norris from the Scripps Institute of Oceanography conducted research that shows that overall cloud changes since 1952 have had a net cooling effect on Earth (Evan and Norris 2012).

The atmosphere is mostly kept reasonably warm for the survival of humans by water vapour and the Earth's hydrosphere.

At night when the sun goes down the temperatures are kept slightly warmer if there is cloud cover. Hence colder starry nights when there is no cloud cover. However the cloud temperature effect on our climate is complex and overall NASA has found a net cooling effect of increased cloud cover. **NASA's Earth Radiation Budget Experiment has identified low clouds as being responsible for 60 per cent of the cooling of the Earth by clouds.**

Clouds are very important as so far their effects have not been included in any climate temperature models (NASA facts 1999). Cloud cover is predicted to increase as the cosmic ray flux rises. Why are we discussing clouds in our hypothesis about an ice age Britain?

The problem with clouds is twofold. Firstly the IPCC has not included cloud cover in any of its climate models! Secondly cloud cover serves to reduce global temperatures by reducing solar influx and by the light reflecting albedo effect.

There is a predicted drop in solar activity in the next solar cycles. When solar activity drops it has an effect on magnetic field strength. The magnetic field plays a vital role in shielding Earth from the incessant bombardment of intergalactic cosmic rays. Therefore when the magnetic field weakens more cosmic rays will enter our atmosphere instead of being deflected. This increase in cosmic ray input has been hypothesised to enable clouds to form more easily.

Therefore when the Sun starts to go inactive the decrease in the magnetic field strength will allow more cosmic rays to enter our atmosphere. These cosmic rays seed cloud formation.

Therefore more cosmic rays equates to more global cloud cover. These cosmic rays are also harmful to health and may contribute to high radiation exposure in air pilots and frequent fliers.

Reflectivity of clouds

The conventional view of climate scientists, as expressed in the reports of the Intergovernmental Panel on Climate Change, is that most of the warming of the Earth's surface over the last few decades is down to the atmospheric build-up of manmade greenhouse gases such as carbon dioxide.

Henrik Svensmark of the National Space Institute in Denmark believes that the cosmic rays and the sun's fluctuating magnetic fields may also play a major role in both warming and cooling. Cosmic rays are charged particles arriving from space or the sun. The intergalactic cosmic rays have been accelerated to speeds faster than any particles in accelerators here on Earth. Galactic cosmic rays are thought to be caused by distant explosions of supernova.

Svensmark has found a strong correlation between these cosmic rays and Earth's climate. The Danish group has reproduced the Earth's atmosphere in the laboratory showing how clouds might be seeded by incoming cosmic rays. The team believes that fluctuations in the cosmic ray flux caused by changes in solar activity could play a role in climate change.

His graphs show an exact correlation between cooler temperatures and cosmic ray influx. His team has found that cosmic rays that can influence the planet's climate by cooling the atmosphere. It is certainly a paradigm shift to consider that earth's climate may be partly influenced by factors from outer space!

Cosmic ray flux is also affected by the Sun's output. When the Sun becomes active cosmic rays decrease and the converse applies. When the sun becomes quiescent then cosmic rays increase. The diagram below charts a steady increase in cosmic rays.

Diagram Credit: Spaceweather.com

A remarkably good fit has been found between measured increases of cosmic rays and measured decreasing temperatures.

According to the Danish astrophysicist Henrik Svensmark the cosmic rays seed the cooling clouds by ionizing molecules in Earth's atmosphere. The low-lying clouds then have the effect of cooling the Earth further by reflecting incoming sunshine back out to space.

The Sun's magnetic field deflect cosmic rays away from the Earth, when solar activity is high leading to global warming. Conversely, Earth becomes cooler when solar activity is low.

I have recently purchased an excellent book that is selling on Amazon by one of my favourite scientists, the late Nigel Calder. Many will remember Nigel Calder as the editor of New Scientist magazine. Henrik Svensmark and Nigel Calder have written a book about their theory of cooling cosmic rays *"The Chilling Stars: a New Theory of Climate Change"* published in 2007.

Svensmark and Calder have shown by their research that cosmic rays have far more effect on the climate than carbon dioxide emissions. Henrik Svensmark, is Director of Climate Research at the Danish National Space Centre.

His studies show that there is a strong correlation between cosmic rays and the formation of aerosols of the type that seed clouds. The authors assert that solar activity is primarily responsible for temperature variation and global climate.

The Sun can affect the amount of cosmic rays reaching our atmosphere via deflection of the magnetic fields. More solar activity leads to fewer cosmic rays. Conversely less solar activity leads to more cosmic rays. The cosmic rays influx then serves to enhance cloud formation. As the sunspot activity lessens, the solar wind diminishes leading to more cosmic rays reaching our atmosphere.

The cosmic rays help to seed the clouds which in turn reflect more heat away from the Earth's surface. Even if a cloud looks dark grey from below the cloud will always appear bright white from above.

The Sun's heliosphere repels intergalactic cosmic rays. The Sun's magnetic field repels the intergalactic cosmic rays from Earth. When the magnetic field weakens, more cosmic rays can enter Earth's atmosphere. There are signs that our magnetic field may be weakening and this could allow more chilly cosmic rays to arrive.

Cosmic rays are ultra- fast proton particles that would threaten life, if not for the shielding of our planet's atmosphere and magnetic field. Cosmic rays create cloud condensation nuclei. Therefore they facilitate cloud formation. Man made pollutants also facilitate this seeding of clouds and so the effect is being amplified. Aerosols in the atmosphere from ships seed clouds adding to the cooling effects from cosmic rays.

Other scientists concur with the cosmic rays affect climate. Professor Jaworowski also believes that the climate is going to get colder rather than warmer in the coming future. He has discovered a close correlation between global temperatures and the intensity of cosmic ray flux. Jaworoski states that solar cycles and cosmic rays influence climate. He is not at all convinced about the role of carbon dioxide (Jaworowski 2004).

There is no doubt that clouds that are induced by cosmic rays have a huge effect on global temperatures. Clouds that appear white on top will provide a reflective albedo effect. It is also interesting to note that the cooling effects of cloud cover have not been included in any of the IPCC climate models! An astronomical study claims to have found a perfect fit between phanerozoic eon temperature and cosmic ray influx.

The team studied iron meteorites. They found fluctuations in cosmic ray flux reaching the Earth can explain 66% of the temperature variance over the past 520 million years! (Shaviv and Veiser 2003).

NASA reported that a powerful cosmic ray storm reached Earth in 2016 and there was speculation that it could interfere with mobile phone reception. Cosmic ray storms could be a portent of a new ice age. Reports in spaceweather.com found that cosmic rays are intensifying. Neutron monitors around the Arctic Circle are recording an increase in cosmic rays. Helium balloons launched over California have found a similar increase. Could this increase in cosmic rays help explain recent stormy weather events?

Measurements show that someone flying back and forth across the USA, just once, can absorb as much ionizing cosmic radiation as given by three dental X-rays. Likewise, cosmic rays can affect mountain climbers, and astronauts on board the International Space Station.

If our cosmic rays do increase as our ice age approaches frequent fliers may get an extra dose of ionising radiation. The path of the Sun through the spiral arms of the Milky Way exposes the Earth to varying intensities of cosmic rays. This passage of our planet through dusty spiral arms in our Milky Way may also explain the onset of ice ages.

One should perhaps expect climatic variations while we roam the galaxy. The density of cosmic ray sources in the galaxy is not uniform. Cosmic rays are concentrated in the galactic spiral arms. Cosmic rays arise arises from supernovae, that are predominantly the end product of massive stars, which form and die primarily in spiral arms.

Each time we cross a galactic arm, we should expect a colder climate or a major ice age. This idea ties in with the cosmic space dust theory of ice ages. Some of the global warming witnessed over the past century could be attributable to the increased solar activity that has diminished the cosmic ray flux reaching Earth.

Tracks of natural cosmic rays have been made visible by a detector at CERN in Geneva. CERN is the European Organisation for Nuclear Research and is home to projects such as the Large Hadron Collider particle accelerator. This underground circular accelerator recently discovered the Higgs Boson or God particle, so called as it is thought to give rise to all matter and mass. Some scientists voiced concerns over the very high speeds being used in the experiment and one even said that it might create a dangerous black hole!!

However CERN would like to see if mini black holes arise, in order to explore new theories about our universe. CERN`s website says that If micro black holes do appear in the collisions created by the LHC, they would disintegrate rapidly, in around 10^{-27} seconds. They would decay into supersymmetric particles, creating events containing an exceptional number of tracks in our detectors, which we would easily spot.

Finding new particles would open the door to yet unknown possibilities about how our inverse works. If they created a big bang would a new universe be born which then proceeded to replace our present universe?

CERN has vigorously denied that the strong magnetic fields generated by the accelerator can affect weather or cause earthquakes here on Earth! Neither will a black hole be generated that will proceed to gobble up our planet!

The Earth`s magnetic field may play a vital part in the onset of ice ages. This is because a weaker magnetic field can allow more cloud forming cosmic rays to penetrate. CERN may provide useful data to track the incoming cosmic rays.

Feeble solar activity and a weak heliosphere both coincide with increases of cosmic rays. Radio carbon 14 in samples on Earth is used to measure these cosmic rays. There is a theory that the galactic centre of our galaxy the Milky Way might be a source of super powerful cosmic rays. The galactic centre is 23, 000 light years away in the constellation of Sagittarius.

The Voyager Missions measured cosmic rays. Voyager found that these highly energetic rays may be increasing in our solar system. This could be due to our solar system passing through an energetic part of the galaxy.

Our solar system is not stationary and moves along and sometimes enters regions of dense interstellar matter. It is possible that a cosmic ray bombardment might originate from the galactic centre in line with the Mayan predictions of a harvesting of souls. It is also thought that a giant black hole lurks in the galactic centre.

The ozone layer may also be damaged by energetic cosmic rays. The Montreal Protocol was enacted to protect the ozone layer and banned ozone destroying chemicals. Other scientists are concerned that rocket launches may be destroying our ozone layer.

Professor Darin Toohey of University of Colorado, Boulder, believes that rocket emissions are worse than CFC`s. These chlorofluorocarbons were banned by the Montreal Protocol to protect the ozone layer. However Professor Toohey feels that a few NASA rocket launches will undo all of the good work from banning CFC`s.

A Canadian astrophysicist from the University of Waterloo believes that cosmic rays have caused most of the damage to the ozone layer. He has found a correlation between cosmic ray intensity and the destruction of ozone. Canadian scientist Qing- Bin Lu is convinced that 100 per cent of Antarctic ozone loss is due to the energetic cosmic rays that interact with the chlorofluorocarbons.

Therefore the primary instigator of the ozone depletion might be the cosmic rays originating from the galactic centre. I am sure the ancient Mayans would be pleased with a theory that aligns with their theory of the galactic heart!

If an ice age is due one might expect the cosmic rays to increase and the ozone layer to diminish. The ozone layer is vital for life on Earth as without it most plants and crops would perish resulting in mass starvation. A NASA experiment with a basil pot plant found the plant turned brown and died when exposed to ultra violet light without protective ozone.

Without the ozone layer protecting us we would soon become blind from radiation induced cataracts. Staggering blind people would roam the Earth searching for food in a zombie style apocalypse.

As the vegetation continued to die the oxygen levels would reduce by half. Without oxygen human life as we know it ceases to exist though primitive anaerobic life forms might survive.

An aerospace engineer claims to have discovered that the ozone depletion is far worse than we are being told. According to the engineer we have only a few years before the ozone layer vanishes! This concern ties in with those of other scientists who fear that our ozone layer is being shredded by rocket launches.

It does seem strange that we are now seeing noctilucent clouds in the skies of Great Britain. In 2018 Imperial College London found that ozone is decreasing in lower latitudes in locations away from the Poles. This finding is very worrying. This might explain the increase in the noctilucent clouds that have been observed at lower latitudes.

HESS Observatory, is an international collaborative venture. This group confirms that the galactic centre of our Milky Way is a source of energetic cosmic rays. Think of Hawking radiation escaping form a black hole!

Galactic core outbursts are possibly the most energetic phenomenon in the universe. The black hole produces super energetic cosmic rays that are accelerated at speeds 100 times that of the particle accelerator, the Large Hadron Collider at CERN. Cosmic rays have energies of up to 100 teraelectronvolts (TeV). To reiterate, cosmic rays are thought to seed clouds and therefore facilitate snow storms.

The rays are also produced by remnants of super nova and pulsars. If a super cosmic ray bombardment arrived it could help trigger the ice age by seeding massive snow storms.

The term galactic superwave was coined by the astronomer Paul LaViolette who is president of the Starburst Foundation. He discovered that galactic superwaves are emitted every 13,000 and 26,000 years. Some scientists believe that in the past huge galactic superwaves have arrived from this region causing massive climate changes on Earth.

Ionisation from intense cosmic rays leads to a depletion of the ozone layer. High levels of ionising radiation in the stratosphere lead to decreased levels of protective ozone. This depletion results in a global cooling.

A high volume of cosmic rays seeds clouds and could trigger a snowblitz on Earth. Some scientists speculate that a galactic superwave is already on its way to Earth and may cause a deadly ice age. The idea that a black hole from the galactic centre could trigger an ice age on Earth is certainly very strange and spooky!

Chapter 6: Our Dimming Skies

As our skies become more polluted they facilitate global dimming. The term global dimming was first used by Gerry Stanhill an English scientist who worked in Israel. Stanhill observed a huge drop in solar radiation from the 1950`s to the present time. He published a paper in 2001 showing that he had observed a 22 per cent fall in solar radiation in Israel.

He then replicated this finding by taking measurements from all over the globe. Everywhere he found the exact same result. Stanhill used pans filled with water to observe the evaporation times under daylight. The rate of water evaporation has been slowing down, which is consistent with global dimming and global cooling. The published paper of the new global dimming concept aroused concern over man`s polluting activities (Stanhill et al, Climatic Change 2004).

Man is polluting the planet and we have yet to see whether this may hasten the onset of our major ice age. Once again, as in the days of London pea soupers, our skies are becoming murkier and smog laden. The dire pollution has recently led the London Mayor Sadiq Khan to call for a ban on woodburning stoves and diesel cars in the capital city.

Certainly there are thousands of deaths each year now linked to air pollution. The Clean Air Act of 1956 banned open fires after the deadly smog of 1952 that killed many London citizens. These days the seminal Clean Air Acts are all but redundant as homeowners are encouraged to install these woodburning stoves! As a result thousands are dying from asthma, bronchitis and heart disease linked to the polluted air.

Recently Stanhill`s global dimming water evaporation results have been replicated by Australian scientists who used a different way to measure the incoming radiation. A satellite array around the Earth is recording worrying falls in levels of solar radiation reaching the surface. A shocking fall of 37 per cent was recorded over Hong Kong.

If this dramatic trend of decreasing solar radiation or insolation continues this could facilitate a return to an ice age. The main cause of this accurately measured global dimming is thought to be air pollution, from particulate pollution dirty emissions such as untreated vehicle exhausts and open wood or coal fires.

In 1974 Time Magazine carried a front page article warning that burning too much coal in open fires could lead to a new ice age. This is due to hazy particulate pollution blocking out the sun's rays. The idea that hazy pollution can prevent sun's warming rays from getting through has been known for a long time in scientific circles. Indeed before our present day zeitgeist of anthropogenic global warming. many scientists in the 1970's voiced concern over the imminent ice age.

However we need to recall that the Solar and Heliospheric Observatory,

SOHO, mission also recorded a drop in the actual output of the sun by 0.015 per cent. This fall in irradiance was measured by the Virgo instrument. This depicts a huge fall in solar output and might also account for global dimming. The observed dimming has measurable differences across the globe.

The dimming was observed to be more severe in the Northern Hemisphere and over countries like China and India. The skies over Malaysia are very dim due to abundant use of open wood fires for cooking. There is no doubt that any decrease in sunlight reaching the surface will have a negative impact on crop yields. Less sunlight results in less energy for crops to turn carbon dioxide and water into the nutrients needed for plant growth.

The ongoing CLOUD experiment at CERN is providing new data about human activities and their effect on cloud formation. The scientists in Geneva are studying cloud seeding from emitted aerosols from sulphur dioxide and other man made industrial emissions. There is no doubt that humans are polluting the skies. This anthropogenic airborne pollution may lead to a global dimming effect and this topic will now be discussed.

Global dimming is caused by sulphur aerosols that reflect sunlight back into space. Pollutants become nuclei to seed cloud droplets. It has been observed that this seeding of pollutants leads to a greater rainfall over busy cities. Polluting vehicles make the dimming worse. Diesel emissions and burning wood in open fires cause both pollution and dimming.

Diesel vehicles have caused tens of thousands of premature deaths each year here in the United Kingdom. The PM2.5 particulates from diesel are also linked with preterm births worldwide (Malley et al 2017).

Diesel cars were given tax breaks by our Government in the belief it would save carbon emissions and prevent global warming. All of the extra pollution from ill conceived Government policies will simply exacerbate the trend for global cooling. NASA recently announced that it had found the most polluted skies over England, Europe, New York, Hong Kong and China from its satellite data.

Very high levels of nitrogen dioxide have been observed and these emissions are very harmful to health. The nitrogen dioxide emissions are coming mostly from vehicles such as the older polluting diesel cars. Diesel cars were promoted heavily in the U.K. as a low carbon and clean alternative!

This is one small example of how confused the policy makers are becoming. Diesel was given a tax break for being low in carbon dioxide. Since carbon dioxide, a non toxic gas, was designated as a pollutant diesel was preferred.

Particulate air pollution in Beijing is providing a cooling canopy of air pollution. China has made the transition from rickshaw to motor car very rapidly. The result is a toxic nightmare of pollution. China does not have the advanced coal power stations that remove particulates using chimney stack scrubbers .China needs to do more to remove the burnt by products. Recently China has made progress in doing this. However the main problem seems to the countless factories that burn coal and let the untreated emissions escape.

Such emissions will appear a murky brownish colour and will be full of sulphur dioxide. Opaque sulphur aerosols act as powerful global cooling agents.The sulphur aersosls now polluting China`s skies burn the lungs of Chinese citizens.

These aerosols are similar to those produced by volcanic eruptions. When sulphur dioxide combines with water it produces an acid rain that kills vegetation.Japan is concerend the acid rain might ruin their crops. Japan has even offered to pay for the desulphurisation equipment needed for China`s coal plants!

China is now making big steps to install desulphurisation equipment in all of its chimney stacks but still lags far behind. China may decommission all of its coal plants soon to remedy the pollution problem. This pollution haze is unlikely contribute to global warming however as has been wrongly asserted. Science journalists broadcasting on Channel 4 News announced incorrectly that the smogs will lead to global warming.

Most likely the dense smogs are acting in a similar way to a geo-engineered sunshield. This cooling effect has led many climate modellers to try and estimate by how much this sulphur induced cooling haze from China will offset any hypothesised carbon dioxide induced warming. Global dimming, it is hoped, may counteract some of the hypothesised anthropogenic warming. Of course if our ice age is about to arrive, any cooling from the global dimming will make the situation a lot worse!

The concept of a nuclear winter is a good example of a catastrophic global dimming. If several nuclear bombs were simultaneously detonated life would die out, skies would darken, crops would fail and a new ice age would dawn. Pollution particles help seed clouds.

Every water droplet in a cloud needs a particle to seed itself around. Ions become attached to particles and act as cloud condensation nuclei. Negative ions, or electrons, collect dust particles as they rise upwards.

The process of cloud seeding has actually been replicated in the laboratory. These particulate seeded clouds then become more reflective than usual. This in turn results in more solar radiation becoming reflected back into cold space. It is of great concern to learn that some scientists wanted to add *more* of these particles into the atmosphere in order to geo-engineer a canopy to further cool the globe.

Some climate scientists have theorized that aircraft **contrails** or vapour trails are implicated in global dimming, but the constant flow of air traffic previously meant that this could not be tested. The total shutdown of **civil air traffic** during the three days following the **September 11, 2001 attacks** afforded a unique opportunity to observe the climate when absent from the effect of contrails.

An increase in **diurnal** temperature variation of over 1 °C (1.8 °F) was observed in some parts of the U.S. This finding proves that aircraft contrails lower daytime temperatures and are causing global dimming (Travis, et al 2002).

Aerosols and other particulates absorb solar energy and reflect sunlight back into space. The pollutants can also **become nuclei** for cloud droplets. Water droplets in **clouds coalesce** around the particles. Increased pollution causes more particulates and thereby creates clouds consisting of a greater number of smaller droplets. The smaller droplets make clouds more **reflective,** so that more incoming sunlight is reflected back into space.

In 1971 Dr. Stephen H. Schneider from the National Center for Atmospheric Research in Boulder, Colorado, claimed that pollution would soon *reduce* the global temperature by 3.5°C. The National Science Board of the U.S. National Science Foundation announced that "The present time of high temperatures should be drawing to an end leading into the next glacial age."

As a postdoctoral fellow at NASA's **Goddard Institute for Space Studies, Stephen Schneider** decided to examine whether the particulates that cool would counteract the carbon dioxide green house effect. In 1971, Schneider was lead author of a paper in

Science titled "Atmospheric Carbon Dioxide and Aerosols".

This paper used a model to examine the competing effects of cooling from aerosols and hypothetical warming effects from CO_2. The paper concluded that mankind's injection of particulate matter in the atmosphere could make the air four times more opaque. The team's calculations suggest the aerosols would result in a *decrease* in global temperature by as much as 3.5 degrees.

Therefore the team decided to favour nuclear power as a future source of energy to prevent the cooling sulphur emissions that might lead to an ice age! These days we have the *exact opposite* scenario whereby some authors favour nuclear power to prevent global warming!

The politician Ed Davey came to Oxford to talk about his work at the Department of Energy and Climate Change (DECC). He spoke about the work his department was doing to insulate more of Britain's chilly homes.

He also spoke of the cleanup operations at nuclear power plant Sellafield which was formerly known as the Windscale plant. However when I asked him about the budget allocated to clean up Sellafield he answered truthfully that £billions of taxpayer funds were being spent cleaning up radioactive waste.

It seemed that most of the department's budget was being spent on Sellafield decontamination. It was a moment of revelation as I realised that nuclear power could not be the solution of our energy needs. Surely this was a galling example of the hidden costs of nuclear power. Paradoxically many so called green environmentalists are calling for nuclear to be favoured as a low carbon source of energy. It may be low in carbon but it is still frighteningly high in radioactive isotopes!

The total costs to clean up Sellafield have been projected to total £53bn. The Nuclear Decommissioning Authority estimates that the site will be clear by the year 2120. Yet it seems that we have not learnt a lesson about expensive nuclear power as this country now proposes to build the most expensive nuclear power plant in the world at Hinkley Point. Nuclear power is both hideously expensive and potentially lethal to the environment.

Japan was shaken to its core on March 11 2011 by a huge earthquake that caused a tsunami to rise up and hurtle towards the supposedly protected shores of Japan.

The floodwall levees were breached and the waters gushed over land with a frightening ferocity. The magnitude 9 earthquake was so huge that it was reported that the entire globe wobbled slightly on its axis. NASA reported that the Earth had shifted slightly on its figure axis leading to a shorter day by 1.8 microseconds.

Amazingly the effects of the earthquake were felt all over the globe and even affected an ice shelf in Antarctica. The Sulzberger Ice Shelf in Antarctica was shaken by the travelling ripple and large chunks broke off that were the size of a city such as Manhattan. Satellite images showed large chunks of ice floating off into the sea shortly after the magnitude 9 quake. This massive earthquake even sent shock waves into our atmosphere. The effect created electrically charged ripples 220 miles high up in the atmosphere.

   The perils of constructing nuclear facilities in an earthquake zone were demonstrated by damage caused to the Japanese nuclear plant at Fukushima. The legacy of Fukushima lives on as a chilling reminder of the dangers of nuclear power. Greenpeace issued a report saying that the contamination from the damaged Fukushima Daiichi plant will last for centuries as it is distributed via the Pacific Ocean through various plant and marine food chains (Greenpeace press release March 2016).

The reason for this digression on nuclear power safety is to highlight the danger of trying to curb carbon emissions. Green authors such as George Monbiot, Mark Lynas and even James Lovelock feel that we must have supposedly "low carbon" nuclear power on the table in order to avoid a catastrophic global warming event. Even the premise that nuclear power is "low carbon" has been called into doubt by a recent study published in the Ecologist in 2015.

The idea that nuclear power might possibly be designated as low carbon was researched by Professor Keith Barnham. The detailed report found that there is no consensus on the carbon footprint of nuclear power and no agreement on the lifetime carbon emissions generated by nuclear power stations.

So called "low carbon" nuclear is in fact high in carbon emissions as well as high plutonium. A lot of the carbon emissions are incurred during the construction phase as concrete is held to be a high carbon substance. Therefore it seems that the pursuit of low carbon nuclear is somewhat misguided.

Despite my grave misgivings I do feel that nuclear power would be invaluable during ice age conditions as a lot of energy would be needed. Mankind will need a huge investment in energy infrastructure and power plants to cope with such a drop in temperatures.

Although as an environmentalist I am against nuclear power, it may have to an option on the icy table. The

Northern Hemisphere may struggle to meet its energy needs and this topic is discussed later in this book.

Did Stephen Schneider make a mistake when saying it would be preferable to favour nuclear power over fossil fuels? Schneider was undoubtedly correct in his assertion that sulphur aerosols act as cooling agents in global temperatures. Let us not forget either that Schneider favoured nuclear power to help prevent the ice age.

Schneider later became concerned about anthropogenic warming along with scientists in the IPCC (Intergovernmental Panel on Climate Change). I think his early idea of an ice age was on the right track and that safely maintained nuclear may prove useful during the ice age.

In the mid-1980s, **Atsumu Ohmura** a geography researcher at the **Swiss Federal Institute of Technology,** found that solar radiation striking the Earth's surface had declined by more than ten per cent. Many experiments have been carries out worldwide on the evaporation of water from flat pans exposed to sunlight. These experiments all show that the rate of water evaporation is slowing, which is consistent with a global dimming hypothesis.

It could also tie in with a phase of the Milankovitch cycle of decreased insolation as Earth tilts away from the Sun on its axis.

Certainly the pan evaporation experiments do not support the global warming hypothesis. Indeed the converse applies and the pan evidence is supporting a global cooling scenario. The decrease in evaporation is consistent with a decrease in sunlight from increasing cloud coverage and global dimming aerosols (*Science* 15 Nov. 2002).

Natural global dimming aerosols are emitted worldwide from volcanic processes. For example there is constant particulate emission from rumblings of volcanoes such as Mauna Loa, the world`s most active volcano in Hawaii. This constant emission of volcanic aerosols consists of both carbon dioxide as well as sulphur aerosols. Indeed natural processes such as volcanic activity do contribute a large amount of atmospheric greenhouse gases.

Yet intriguingly the net effect of volcanic eruptions appears to be one of cooling via a global dimming effect. It is within the realms of probability that a large amount of the present day increase in atmospheric levels of carbon dioxide are the result volcanic emissions from Mauna Loa rather than the activities of man.

However we must not be complacent about the deleterious effect of our polluting activities are having on the atmosphere. The endless launch of test missiles is no doubt contributing to the shredding of our vital ozone layer.

Indeed it has been said that of the present day carbon dioxide in the atmosphere, man is responsible for less than one per cent. The rest of the carbon dioxide is derived from organic processes such as decomposition of plants and ocean dynamics. However one has to realise how powerful is the catalyst effect of carbon dioxide. Carbon dioxide is a vital catalyst which enables all life on earth to flourish. Despite being present in relatively minute quantities a trace gas may have a huge effect.

Our planet would be a barren uninhabited wasteland were it not for carbon dioxide. Despite it comprising only 400 parts per million this important gas enables all photosynthesis and plant respiration to take place on our beautiful planet.

This depicts how a small part of the atmosphere can exert a very large effect. Therefore it is not surprising that some scientists are concerned about rising carbon dioxide levels. Without this trace gas there would be no vegetation and by logical deduction there would be no life on Earth whatsoever.

Therefore despite being in minute quantities this gas has an enormous effect. The burning question is can such a small increase of this life giving gas from man`s activities make such a difference that we may stall the onset of our looming ice age? This is complex but it is possible that black soot deposits on white snow could counteract the albedo effect. This is the one and only possible way that man theoretically might be able to warm the planet.

Indeed this idea to geo-engineer the prevention of an ice age with soot was put forward by the scientist Fred Singer. This distinguished scientist realised that an ice age is coming within 200 years at the very latest. Fred Singer therefore proposed that dirty black soot could be sprinkled on the white pristine snows of Canada to absorb the sun's warming rays. Needless to say most environmentalists would not be pleased at this idea!

Carbon dioxide comes in many forms including dirty polluting hydrocarbons. Some of this dirty black carbon falls as soot on pristine white snow. These dark patches of soot appear dark from space. Since they are dark they can absorb the sun's rays. This absorption of solar energy serves to counteract the albedo effect. Dirty sooty hydrocarbons pollute our skies and are actually be cooling rather than warming our planet.

So here we see that sooty carbon may either warm or cool the planet and its climatic effects are very complex. In its pure form carbon dioxide is an innocuous harmless gas essential to life. However carbon dioxide comes in combinations such as dirty hydrocarbons that pollute our skies and damage our lungs. Hence it is easy to understand how carbon emissions are now considered a bad thing for our planet's ecosystems.

Despite widespread concerns, man is still managing to emit vast clouds of hazy pollution especially in countries such as Malaysia where wood burning for cooking is common. The brown hazy smogs can be clearly seen from satellite photos from space. This Asian brown cloud as it is called, covers much of the Indian Ocean.

It is caused by cooking with open fires using wood. This also creates health problems from the smoke inhaled indoors. Two million die in India alone from this noxious particulate laden pollution. The smoky method of cooking is used because of extreme poverty and of households being unable to afford cleaner methods of cooking.

Yet ironically woodburning stoves are becoming increasingly trendy in wealthy households in the U.K. The misguided belief here is that burning wood, now rebranded as biomass, will help to alleviate global warming and save carbon emissions.

The idea that burning wood is somehow carbon neutral is plainly ludicrous. More than one million British households now have a wood burning stove and more are being installed each year to the detriment of local air quality.

It seems that our Clean Air Act which saved the lives of many Londoners back in the 1950`s is now becoming all but redundant. Back in the 1950`s open fires were very common since central heating did not exist in many homes. This caused the skies of London and other cities to become filled with dark acrid smoke. During foggy periods the skies of London became known as foggy pea soupers. These smogs gave rise to a lot of serious ill health and respiratory illnesses became rife.

The crippling air pollution forced Governments to act and so a Clean Air Act was introduced in 1956.London skies were once filled with smogs from countless open coal or wood fires and chimneys belched out noxious smoke.

Not surprisingly respiratory disease was rife and tuberculosis was very common a century ago up until the 1950`s. The killer smog of London in 1952 was mainly caused by these countless open fires. The terrible toll on public health finally gave rise to the Clean Air Act of 1956. Another Clean Air Act was introduced in 1993.

However these vital protections to our health are now being reversed by Whitehall "climate" legislation. DEFRA has called for rules to be relaxed as the Clean Air Act now conflicts with low carbon energy policy! This new policy means that it is now encouraged to burn wood in fireplaces as it is now supposedly low carbon. In fact wood is not at all low carbon and burning wood will cause serious damage to the health of all local residents. Neither is it acceptable to burn coal in the fireplace for the same reason.

I vividly recall a green energy open day that was held in my street to demonstrate eco energy. It was sunny day with clear blue skies in October. As I walked past the eco open day at the house I saw a jet- black plume of smoke belching out of the chimney that looked and smelt awful. Inside the house were two new woodburners blazing away at full blast with logs inside. This event many years ago got me thinking about burning wood or biomass.

Although it looked very cosy and homely inside, the outside of the street was fast becoming a polluted nightmare and I prayed the eco day would soon end as the acrid choking smoke blew into my kitchen. I appreciate that open fires are lovely to look at. For isolated rural dwellers surrounded by woods, I see no harm in their burning log fires.

However there can be no questioning that log burners will prove useful in America for the self sufficient preppers. If an ice age arrives, those with a supply of wood to burn and a log burner may fare better than those reliant on the national grid.

Survivalists who have ample land and who live in secluded woods can easily afford to burn the fallen wood and will not jeopardise the health of residents. As a last resort, burning wood may be the only means to cook food and to keep warm.

The preppers in America are ready to live off the land and will be able to survive when an apocalypse arrives. When the national grid collapses then clearly people will need to resort to burning wood. When power cuts arrive, burning home gathered wood will help the rural survivalists to survive an ice age. Burning wood to generate heat is fine in isolated areas or countries with vast tracts of available land.

However many studies are now showing just how dangerous burning wood in congested built up areas can be. Wood smoke releases some benzene compounds that are linked with childhood leukaemia. Benzene is a carcinogen that is also found in petrol emissions.

This trend for burning wood for energy is leading to widespread deforestation worldwide. Some of our power stations here in Great Britain have been converted to burn biomass. This is probably not a great environmental policy as the world needs more trees. Furthermore burning wood releases a lot of noxious chemicals linked with cancer, bronchitis and heart disease. Burning wood in a densely populated residential area will lead to respiratory problems and particulate pollution in the neighbourhood. The idea that it is somehow "greener" to burn wood is a contentious one.

A study published by New Scientist showed that inhaling wood smoke for an hour is equal to smoking 100 cigarettes. It is vital that the wood to be burnt is carefully treated and dried but this rarely happens. Burning any old wood will not do and may release deadly dioxins, heavy metals and pesticides.

Sadly many trees are now being destroyed for wood-burners and not being replanted. It seems to be a case of not being able to see the wood for the trees! Burning trees for fuel is not eco-friendly, as trees give out oxygen and take up carbon dioxide. Unlike the inert coal used in power stations, trees are living with leaves. We have precious little ancient woodland left in our country.

Ironically in our bid to be "green" we are now burning more wood than at any time since the Industrial Revolution. The reason we are turning to wood is that we will lose a lot of energy when all of our 15 coal power stations close to conform to an EU directive.

This Directive is known as the European Large Combustion Plant Directive and was instigated by Euro Green MEP`s who hoped that closing coal power stations would stave off an imminent global warming. This premature closure of fully functioning power stations not at the end of their shelf life will likely lead to an energy gap and energy insecurity.

The sad aspect of our power station closures is that it is entirely unnecessary. The coal power stations in the U.K benefited from advanced technology to clean up emissions.

Their chimney stacks had scrubbers that removed most of the particulate pollution that may cause acid rain. There was no harmful pollution around the coal power stations here in the U.K. due to technologically advanced chimney scrubbers that scrubbed the particulate sulphur pollution from the emissions.

I witnessed the Power Station at Didcot, Oxfordshire being blown up. Everyone was cheering as the large towers collapsed but I was aghast. Many years before this futile and pointless destruction the Oxford Mail and Oxford Times had published several of my letters the gist of which was that we should keep Didcot Power station and our other coal power stations. When Didcot power station in Oxfordshire was up and running did it lead to an ambient rise in local temperatures as the warming coal emissions model would predict?

Actually the converse was true. There was a measured statistical increase of a chance of winter snow flurries around the power station! So it seems that the model of carbon dioxide as a warming gas may have been overstated and that we have more to fear from a global cooling caused by our emissions. Did the health of Didcot residents suffer from living near the power plant?

No, it most certainly did not suffer from the clean emissions. Didcot had benefited from advanced technology with chimney stack scrubbers removing all particulate pollution though the carbon dioxide remained. Epidemiologists in Oxfordshire found that residents of Didcot were not only healthier than average but also had a slightly longer life expectancy! The only emissions from our cheap to run power stations were steam and a smidgeon of carbon dioxide.

Instead of closing our vital infrastructure, we could have planted a small copse of trees around each power station. This would have satisfied the need to offset carbon emissions and pleased environmentalists who are concerned about carbon dioxide emissions.

Trees also soak up carbon dioxide lie a thirsty sponge. I wrote to the Government with this suggestion to plant a copse of trees around each power station ear marked for closure to absorb the carbon dioxide from the power stations.

This pragmatic suggestion has not been implemented needless to say! The Government would rather run the risk of power cuts and impose expensive energy from nuclear power on its citizens instead of planting some trees. The closure of coal power stations seems to have become a symbol of our efforts to care for the environment. It is mere gesture politics.

The closure of our desperately needed power stations will lead to power cuts if we do not replace the energy deficit. There are far better ways to look after our precious ecosystems. People can try and cycle instead of driving their car. The worst emissions are undoubtedly those from diesel vehicles that emit particulates and nitrogen dioxide which harm our health.

Blowing up perfectly good power stations to save the planet is the most ludicrous idea that any civilised country has embraced. While it is true that burning raw coal in open fires releases unpleasant pollutants, this is not the case when coal is burnt in our advanced power stations. The irony is that by closing our power stations our skies may become far more polluted and lead to global dimming.

When the power cuts arrive in the future homeowners will increasingly turn to burning wood or untreated coal in their fireplaces to keep warm! Our advanced power station technology to burn coal cleanly for electricity will be replaced with polluting wood stoves and open fires. We are indeed regressing back into the Dark Ages!

If the U.K continues its love affair with burning wood the resulting hazy pollution may create an added risk for dimming the sun`s input. This may further exacerbate any dip in temperatures and encourage the onset of our well overdue ice age.

Many studies have proved that air pollution actually prevents sunlight from reaching us and therefore smogs cool the ambient temperature rather than raise the temperature.

A Channel 4 newscaster recently announced that smog would lead to more global warming and this assertion was incorrect. This cooling effect from aerosols has been demonstrated repeatedly by volcanic eruptions that emit airborne particulate aerosol matter.

The volcanic eruptions of Mount Pinatubo and Tambora resulted in lower temperatures worldwide that are popularly known as the years without a summer. Smogs and dense particulate pollution may harm people, but should not be confused with pure carbon dioxide emissions. Carbon dioxide as a pure gas is both good for plants and ocean life.

Air pollution has repeatedly been shown to lower rather than raise temperatures. For example after the

9/11 air attacks all planes were grounded in New York.

Because the skies were clear of hazy aircraft contrails, the sunlight was able to reach the ground unfiltered. The measured temperatures shot up in New York. This meteorological observation demonstrated that the aircraft contrails are cooling temperatures over cities such as New York. When the ice age arrives, many thriving American cities such as New York will be hit very hard.

Back in 1974 Wilson Clark wrote that "instead of growing warmer, the Earth may enter an ice age as a result of fuel combustion. The combustion of fossil fuels releases large quantities of particulate matter into the atmosphere, which may reflect sunlight away from the Earth, thus cooling the planet". So here we have a climate hypothesis that is diametrically opposed to the present day theory that fossil fuels may cause global warming.

Instead Clark states that these fossil fuel emissions may cause a drop in ambient temperatures and that our industrial activity may cool rather than warm our atmosphere. This seems a far more persuasive argument than the warming hypothesis .

It is interesting to note that just as today there is a scare about global warming , back in the 1970`s there was a similar scare about a global cooling and a coming ice age. The global warming fear has probably become the dominant one since it now has huge financial vested commercial interests backing it.

Either way we should be cleaning our skies. With the amount of air, ship and vehicular traffic, this looks nigh on an impossible task. The last thing we should be doing to keep our skies clean in the U.K is to blow up perfectly good power stations.

We need our infrastructure to keep our society and economy functioning. There are far better ways to ensure our skies are clear. Households should avoid installing a trendy woodburner and avoid burning any fossil fuel such as wood or coal in their fireplace.

Nitrogen Dioxide (NO_2) is a common pollutant in towns and cities, and diesel vehicles are a particular problem. According to think tank Policy Exchange the most recent Euro 6 diesel cars emit more than five times as much NOx as Euro 6 petrol cars. Euro 6 are the latest EU standards for air pollution emissions from cars (European Commission 27/06/2016).

Yet diesel cars were promoted as being good for the environment as they are allegedly low in carbon emissions. This is just one small example of the many scams that have arisen as a result of the carbon dioxide legislation.

Electric cars are the way forward as they emit no particulate pollution. Therefore thousands of lives will be saved. However when the ice age arrives we may need 4 wheel drive versions with extra gripping tyres! Worryingly we might not have enough electricity to charge up the electric vehicles. As the climate cools there may be an energy deficit.

This legislation to promote "low carbon" diesel cars came from the EU and it seems that the EU is causing more harm than good with some of its Directives. Despite this legislation for clean emissions there are around 40,000 premature deaths a year now in the U.K. thought to be caused by air pollution. Far from improving matters the legislation introduced to help prevent global warming is making things worse. This is just one of the examples of how the focus on carbon emissions has resulted in unwise legislation.

The other example that springs to mind is the closure of our non polluting coal power stations in the U.K that did not emit any harmful pollutant. Another example is the fashion for laughably "low carbon" woodburners that are now causing air pollution levels in London not seen since the days of the foggy pea soupers back in the

1950`s . All done in the name of preventing a man made global warming event.

So it seems that some of misguided attempts to lower carbon emissions have resulted in greater air pollution in our cities. DEFRA has called for air quality rules to be relaxed as the Clean Air Act now conflicts with their low carbon energy policy.

This new policy means that it is now encouraged to burn wood in fireplaces as it is now supposedly low carbon! The policy to burn wood was probably introduced to make up for a deficit in energy caused by closing our coal power stations.

Clearer non-polluted skies will lead to greater sunlight radiation reaching Earth and warmer temperatures will boost crop production. Perhaps we should curtail burning fossil fuels to prevent a global cooling rather than a global warming. Whichever climate theory you may subscribe to, it should be imperative that we do not pollute our skies with smogs.

NASA has recently confirmed that the Northern Hemisphere may get cooler as a result of sulphur aerosols and pollution. The Goddard Institute of Space Studies has published a paper by Gavin Schmidt and Kate Marvel showing how aerosols cool temperatures. This theory of cooling aerosols was discussed in the early 1990`s by climate scientist Antony Milne in his excellent book "Earth`s Changing Climate" which I highly recommend.

NASA has only recently decided to include pollution in their climate models. It looks as if their conclusion that burning fossil fuels may cool the Northern Hemisphere might be the most accurate deduction of their climate modelling. NASA says that carbon dioxide is distributed evenly around the globe to cause a uniform warming effect. That is factually incorrect even according to NASA`s own satellites!! The carbon dioxide does not mix uniformly in the air and instead gathers in pockets before falling to the ground as it is a heavy gas.

  NASA has satellites photos showing this patchiness of carbon dioxide around the globe. NASA cannot therefore state that carbon dioxide is distributed evenly in the atmosphere!! The satellites pictures show as clear as daylight that the carbon dioxide is not evenly distributed at all and in many parts of the atmosphere it is completely absent! This one single fact alone punches a huge hole in the carbon dioxide warming hypothesis.

Kate Marvel who is the lead author of the cooling aerosol study writes that the aerosols are more or less confined to the Northern Hemisphere, where most of us live and emit pollution. There is proportionately more land in the Northern Hemisphere than the Southern Hemisphere. Land reacts quicker than the ocean does to these atmospheric changes (Marvel, Schmidt et al 2016).

One of the reasons that burning fossil fuels such as coal can cause cooling is that it will release sulphur dioxide. However when treated fossil fuels are burnt in a coal power station the sulphur dioxide will be removed by chimney scrubbers and this problem will be avoided.

China however is burning a lot of untreated coal. NASA has said that China is one of the most polluted countries in the world and the smog can be seen from space satellites. Clean transparent air allows sunlight to reach us warming our skin and improving our mood.

Imagine the dawn of the new ice age when the sun goes dim and skies are leaden and grey. This is a real prospect for us in the not too distant future. Meanwhile some climate scientists are convinced that there is a need to engineer some sort of a cooling sunshade over the Earth to prevent global warming! Some mad -cap scientists are now exploring ways to further cool the planet! This topic of geo-engineering the climate will now be discussed.

Chapter 7: The Hazards of Geo-engineering our Climate

  Scientists have long known how to seed clouds with silver iodide in order to make it rain heavily. In 1946 a scientist named Irving Langmuir working for General Electric discovered how to make rain in the laboratory. Silver iodide was found to be a good nucleating agent for the seeding of rain clouds. The science of geo-engineering the weather had arrived.

  When it comes to tampering with our weather one should adopt a precautionary approach. A cloud seeding experiment was once conducted in Devon using silver iodide as the cloud seeding agent.

This military experiment resulted in torrential rains leading to flash floods, mudslides and deaths. On August 15, 1952, one of the worst flash floods ever to have occurred in Britain swept through the Devon village of Lynmouth.

Thirty five people died as a torrent of 90m tons of water and thousands of tons of rock poured off saturated Exmoor and into the village destroying homes, bridges, shops and hotels. New evidence from previously classified government files suggests that a team of international scientists working with the RAF was experimenting with artificial rainmaking in southern Britain in the same week and could be implicated. Certainly this was a suspicious deluge of rain that appeared to come from nowhere.

Later an American scientist admitted taking part in Project Cumulus to make it rain hard in Britain at that time. Today it is reported that cloud seeding takes place over ski resorts to ensure good snow cover. Japan has used seeding for extra rain to enhance crop production. Colorado ski resorts often use this method to boost snow cover. The Wyoming Weather Modification Pilot Project indicates that snow fall can be increased by up to 15 per cent using this method.

So it seems that man can indeed influence the weather and therefore the anthroposphere is a real concept. Recently scientists have been turning their attention to ambitious geo-engineering projects to cool our entire planet! No doubt the residents of Norway and freezing Russia will be most appreciative! Since it has been shown from geologic records that a very small change of insolation can dramatically cool our planet, this gigantic sun canopy could trigger a massive ice age.

   I once attended a public climate change lecture in the Oxford Physics Department where scientists were discussing various ideas of how to cool the planet with carbon capture and geo-engineering.

   There was a futuristic and mind boggling proposal to engineer a giant sun canopy shield over our atmosphere to keep our planet cool! The main "solution" to cool our world is to inject reflective sulphur based aerosol particles high up into the atmosphere. These particles will reflect the sun`s light and heat back into space , in much the same way that volcanic ash cools the skies as discussed in the previous chapter.

The National Center for Atmospheric Research suggested in 2006 that sulphur aerosols should be injected into the atmosphere to keep the temperature down. Tom Wigley proposed that the amount of sulphate aerosols should be of a similar quantity to those aerosols ejected by the volcanic eruption of Mount Pinatubo in 1991 which cause temperatures to fall in the region. When the volcano erupted in 1991 the following year temperatures fell.

This is clearly a vast amount of airborne matter to be put into our stratosphere. Tom Wigley thinks that this geo-engineering project will be able to "buy us time" in which to deal with the challenges of global warming. Wigley convinced himself that geo-engineering the atmosphere would prevent a carbon dioxide induced temperature rise. Or maybe he just wanted to make a profit! This worrying project shows just how far scientists are willing to go in order to combat the perceived anthropogenic warming.

It is known that huge amounts of sulphur based aerosol will lead to a lot of damage to our precious ozone layer. We are fortunate that Wigley`s proposal to mimic the output of a yearly volcanic eruption did not come to fruition. It is thought that one of the reasons for the cool temperatures of the little Ice Age could have been due to five volcanic eruptions during that time.

The respected scientist Nigel Calder has voiced his cynicism over the alleged warming properties of carbon dioxide. Calder proposes that the greenhouse effect of carbon dioxide levels off after a certain point of saturation has been reached.

So rather than a hockey stick we have a level graph. In other words more carbon dioxide does not equate to more warming. It is as simple as that. Therefore, according to the late Nigel Calder, most, if not all, of the accepted models of warming by carbon dioxide are incorrect.

This assertion is given further weight by the observation that although carbon dioxide levels continue to rise to the present day level of around 400 parts per million the observed global temperatures are not rising in tandem with the measured CO_2. In other words although carbon dioxide is a valuable greenhouse gas that has a benign influence its effects are limited. Therefore the whole industry that has sprung up around saving carbon emissions may turn out to have been a red herring.

However it has been a lucrative endeavour for those in the low carbon business loop! Meanwhile a whole generation of scientists are blindly going down a dead end in their quest to geo-engineer a cooler planet. The main problem facing our survival is the onset of a major ice age.

By the time this overdue ice age has arrived it may be too late and whole swathes of the Northern Hemispheric population may be wiped out. Even worse is the realisation that to date all of our efforts to make our world safer have in fact made it a far more dangerous place.

So far all of the proposed ideas to geo-engineer our climate, revolve around the need to cool planet Earth. Not one proposal has emerged to geo-engineer our climate in the face of a bitter ice age. However the USA has a military project called HAARP which some conspiracy theorists believe is to heat the ionosphere in the advent of an ice age.

Some worried Americans are convinced that their Government knows something about a rapid cooling event and that this project is working on a plan to avert a catastrophe.

This is speculation however as the HAARP (High Frequency Active Auroral Research Programme) project was designed to study radio transmission signals high in the ionosphere for a military purpose. HAARP did use an ionospheric heater as part of the research though it is unlikely it had anything to do with preparing for an ice age.

Another project named EISCAT involves an ionospheric heater and took place in Norway. HAARP is loosely based on this work. EISCAT stands for European Incoherent Scatter Scientific Association. Again the research involves radar signals high in the ionosphere. I am presuming the purpose of these studies is to understand the interaction of solar influences on radar. I do not fully understand how an ionospheric heater is being used as I am not an expert in this field.

It seems that the ionospheric heat pump studies plasma turbulence using high frequency transmitters that reflect radio waves back to the ground from the ionosphere. Whether this device can be used to heat the atmosphere is purely speculative.

However it seems apparent that there are strange experiments taking place in the skies above us .The Oxford scientist Pak -Han Wong is advising that we adopt a precautionary and ethical approach to geo-engineering experiments.

Not one geo-engineering proposal to date involves warming the planet to prepare for an ice age. I have to admit that I was concerned on hearing of the proposed giant sunshades as in 2007 I had already considered the prospect of an impending ice age. There are many plans in the pipeline for carbon capture projects.

However some scientists feel that carbon capture technology may prove prohibitively expensive. The Earth's own carbon cycle already does a good job at capturing and recycling carbon. Carbon dioxide becomes carbonic acid when falling as rain and this in turn becomes calcium carbonate and so on.

I attended a climate conference in Oxford that discussed carbon capture and the engineers mostly agreed that it would be prohibitively expensive. At the post drinks reception I chatted to a few engineers and despite the free alcoholic drinks they seemed quite alarmed at the some of the plans to capture carbon dioxide from power plants.

One of the engineers was very worried and said that the proposal to capture carbon would be ridiculously expensive and was not an economically viable engineering proposition!

Fast forward ten years to the year 2018 and the sensible warnings from engineers have been completely ignored as expensive carbon capture pipelines are planned for Drax power station. An example of a carbon capture and storage power plant is the Petra Nova plant in Houston. This large post combustion CCS (Carbon Capture and Storage) facility is costing billions of dollars!

The process of adding the carbon capture and storage doubles the cost of the power plant. It is not necessary to do this to avert global warming either. However some "good" may yet come out of the expensive upgrades at power plants. The carbon dioxide gas may be used to pump out crude oil it seems in a process called enhanced oil delivery.

Other geo-engineering proposals include dropping large amounts of iron filings into the oceans. The iron will encourage the growth of phytoplankton and lead to a green algal bloom. The plankton will then remove excess carbon dioxide and theoretically this will help to cool the planet. David Biello reports the controversial carbon sink iron experiment in the *Scientific American* (July 19, 2012.).

In 2012 a geo-engineering experiment took place in the ocean that was deemed to have violated United Nations rules and conventions on geo-engineering. An American businessman dumped 100 tons of iron sulphate into the Pacific Ocean on the West coast of Canada. This caused a huge algal bloom of plankton that could be seen from space satellites. The bloom covered an enormous area that was thousands of square miles large. The dumped iron had acted as a giant fertiliser for the plankton.

The reason that business man Russ George conducted this geo-engineering venture was that he hoped to make a fortune from the lucrative carbon credits market. This carbon trading business has been discussed elsewhere in this book. The carbon market has also served the skew the impartial debate on climate change in favour of global warming. As a financier friend of mine once said "always follow the money my dear!"

The theory is that the green plankton will remove carbon dioxide from the atmosphere and so the businessman would make a large profit with carbon credit schemes. However scientists are still debating whether this idea may be harmful to ocean life. There are concerns that experiments such as these could harm ocean eco systems and produce toxic tides of oxygen depleted waters.

The lucrative carbon credit scam was sold to the local community as being of environmental benefit. The villagers were told that the iron filings would enhance their salmon fishing. Legal experts said that the project had violated the UN convention on biological diversity.

All of this tampering and attempts to cool our globe may have catastrophic consequences and lead us into a new ice age even sooner than anticipated. These ice ages are not trivial weather events such as an annoyingly cold winter, but cataclysmic events lasting up to 100, 000 years!

We have more to fear from a massive ice age and should therefore leave the geo-engineering to the proverbial mad cap eccentric scientists! There is a widespread belief that sinister and secretive geo-engineering experiments may already be taking place across the world.

A more likely explanation is that the hazy contrails created by aircraft and ships are reflecting sunlight back and so are incidentally creating a geo-engineering cooling effect that is not intentional. This contrail hypothesis could be corroborated by the fact that when aircraft were grounded during the terrorist attack of 9/11, the local ambient temperatures rose.

Meteorologists measured a localised rise in temperature in New York as the lack of air craft contrails meant that sunlight could reach the ground surface unimpeded. As an aircraft contrail dissipates, it leaves behind an icy haze. The sky may appear cloud free, but the particles are there until they fall out of the atmosphere. The contrail particles scatter the sun's light in a similar way as in the proposed geo-engineering cooling projects.

Therefore since our skies are already full of cooling particles it seems a redundant policy to geo-engineer further light reflecting particles.

Furthermore it is known that these cooling sulphur aerosols can damage the ozone layer.

The ozone layer is vital since it shields us from incoming radiation. Therefore it is of concern to learn that in 2012 two Harvard engineers conducted a geo-engineering experiment over New Mexico. The scientists used a hot air balloon to spray light reflecting sulphur aerosols that were similar to those cooling particulates emitted by volcanoes.

A similar geo-engineering event here in the United Kingdom aroused controversy and was eventually cancelled. The U. K. project was known as SPICE which is the acronym for Stratospheric Particle Injection for Climate Engineering.

SPICE was put to rest after campaigners argued that it could open the door for a large scale implementation of the concept. The project was funded by a large Government grant and Dr. Matthew Watson was the study's lead author. It seems that a dispute over patents and copyright may have been the final straw for the research.

However scientists are still looking at ways of cooling our planet. This is very worrying as the hard data from the geologic record is warning us that our Northern hemisphere is heading for a major glaciation event. This event could arrive sooner than expected and we will not be prepared for it. Do we really need any extra cooling aerosols anyway when there are already so many emissions from volcanic activity and aircraft?

There has been a lot of internet chatter about an alleged Government conspiracy to affect our environment with chemtrails. These chemtrails sprays are thought to be sprayed from aircraft and supposedly look just like the emissions from aircrafts known as contrails.

While researching the nefarious art of geoengineering techniques I did indeed come across experiments that might have given rise to this conspiracy theory. It seems that there are numerous ongoing studies into how to use aircraft to deliver aerosols high into the atmosphere in order to cool our planet.

Most of these aircraft spraying research projects are taking place in

North America which is rather ironic as America has recently suffered from some appallingly cold snowy winters. The press reports show footage of the homeless sitting on top of heating air vents in the streets in Washington DC and struggling to survive. Yet America is home to the most sophisticated research being conducted in how to cool our climate.

A geo=engineering paper on cooling aircraft spray was published in 2010 by Jeffry Pierce titled "Efficient formation of stratospheric aerosol for climate engineering by emission of condensable vapour from aircraft". So it seems that there is a grain of truth in the chemtrail conspiracy theory after all! As the old saying goes "there is no smoke without fire".

Residents in the Mount Shasta county of California are concerned about alleged geo-engineering experiments using aluminium. They believe that aluminium is being sprayed using aircraft and that this toxic metal is getting into their water supply.

They are convinced that aluminium products are being used in an experiment to cool the skies. It is possible that ski companies are behind this spraying if indeed it is taking place. It is a controversial area and there is no agreement yet, but a lingering suspicion remains over the cause of high levels of aluminium salts found on Mount Shasta.

Cooling and polluting emissions are also emitted by cargo ships according to a NASA study. Sulphur based aerosols have been linked with damage to the ozone layer. If the protective ozone layer is damaged it leads to greater radiation levels reaching us. This can damage our health and lead to genetic mutations. Some scientists even speculate that this radiation can lead to a higher risk of ailments such as thrombosis.

Any damage to the ozone layer can cause a hole in the ozone layer. These ozone holes let heat escape and this leads to global cooling. A team of Antarctic scientists think that the giant ozone hole is helping to keep Earth cool and as the hole mends the temperature may climb. Professor John Turner works for the British Antarctic survey and thinks that the polar ice increase may be due to the ozone hole above the South Pole.

The Montreal Protocol in 1989 banned ozone depleting chemicals such as chlorofluorocarbons (CFC`s) worldwide. Scientists hope that the ozone hole may heal by 2050 as a result of this ban. These CFC`s used to be found in spray cans but have now been banned from products such as hairsprays. Either way this ozone hole could be a warning sign of cooling and an ice age.

There are many substances that can harm the ozone layer which is found in the stratosphere. Geo=engineering projects are also aimed at injecting particles into this delicate area.

The appearance of the noctilucent polar stratospheric clouds may also be warning us that all is not well in the ozone layer. In a nutshell the signs are pointing to a dramatic cooling of our stratosphere. I believe that this could be a warning sign that we should start to prepare for an ice age of some description.

Everyone has heard of the term "nuclear winter". The worst case scenario of a nuclear war would be blackened skies that prevent all sunlight from reaching Earth. Even if the nuclear blast did not kill you the resultant nuclear winter would ensure that all plant life would die and we would slowly freeze to death.

The term nuclear winter was first coined by Richard P. Turco who made computer models in 1983 of the sooty debris thrown up by nuclear war. His models suggested a catastrophic cooling if many nuclear weapons are detonated.

The climate scientist Stephen Schneider called this smoky layer a smokeosphere.

His research papers published in 1986 that show a global cooling effect would result .We now have to ask ourselves a question about the atmospheric effects of our nuclear emissions to date. An enormous number of test nuclear bombs have been detonated above the ground. Surely these explosions must be having some sort of effect on our delicate atmosphere?

Since it is known that radioactive fallout can damage the ozone layer it is not unreasonable to question whether our nuclear emissions may have contributed to damage to the stratospheric ozone layer.. The weakening magnetic field is also causing ozone holes to grow larger and these growing holes will ultimately lead to heat loss in our thermosphere.

In February 2017 the North Korean Leader Kim Jong-Un launched a missile to celebrate his Father`s birthday! Missiles are constantly being tested all over the globe by the nuclear powers and we still do not know if these detonations may result in incipient damage to our fragile ozone layer.

We do know however that detonating too many nuclear weapons in one go will lead to a nuclear winter, crop depletion and a severe ice age in the Northern hemisphere. Our skies are becoming progressively dirtier and this can lead to a cooling effect via global dimming.

Oxford has its own geo-engineering programme at the Martin School. On its website it states that its aims "to engage with society about the issues associated with geo-engineering and conduct research into some of the proposed techniques.

The programme does not advocate implementing geo-engineering, but it does advocate conducting research into the social, ethical and technical aspects of geo-engineering. This research must be conducted in a transparent and socially informed manner."

This is mildly reassuring. However the website also states that "geo-engineering is the deliberate, large-scale intervention in the Earth's natural systems to address climate change. Although we believe that society's first priority should be to reduce global carbon emissions, in dealing with climate change it may be wise to consider geo=engineering the climate to reduce the harmful levels of carbon dioxide in the atmosphere."

If we are indeed heading into an ice age the last thing we should be considering is measures to remove carbon dioxide from our atmosphere. Indeed we may perhaps consider the benign though improbable possibility that perhaps some of these greenhouse gas emissions may be stalling our overdue ice age.

If this is the case then we should be exceedingly thankful that carbon dioxide levels are rising slightly to 400 ppm. However we need to remember that more carbon dioxide does not necessarily equate to more warmth. The atmospheric dynamics are far more complex than this simple equation!

Highly respected scientists such as the late Sir Fred Hoyle and Nigel Calder believed that water vapour is a far more important green house gas than carbon dioxide. The respected astronomer demonstrated that as carbon dioxide levels rise, the greenhouse effect starts to diminish in a linear fashion.

So in other words there is an optimum level of carbon dioxide which serves to trap the radiative heat of the sun. After this optimum level of CO_2 is reached any rise in carbon dioxide does not correspond with an analogous rise in the greenhouse effect. Therefore any rises in carbon dioxide above this level will not lead to an exponential rise in temperature from the greenhouse effect.

This deduction is based on atmospheric physics and if it is correct then the logical conclusion is that even if our carbon dioxide levels are rising, as they seem to be at present, this rise will not necessarily lead to a similar rise in temperatures. The staggering conclusion from this assertion is that the linear models of rising carbon dioxide levels and the equivalent linear rises in temperature are probably deeply flawed.

  None of this would probably matter too much were it not for the fact that we are now over due a major ice age. Yet all of our Governmental policies seem to be geared towards a warming event. It is important to remember that an ice age will affect the Northern hemisphere disproportionately as this is where the main land mass lies. This is why I gave the book the title "Ice Age Britain".

Therefore equatorial regions will still enjoy warm and even hot weather as may have happened during previous glacials. The fact that equatorial regions may remain warm does not mean we should ignore our own very cold weather in the North.

We are placing ourselves in a very dangerous situation by ignoring the coming glacial threat to our shores. The Northern Hemisphere is densely populated and we need to prepare ourselves for the fact that the predicted global warming may transpire to be a cooling event that triggers an ice age.

The main greenhouse gas is undoubtedly water vapour. The reason that we hardly ever hear of this fact is probably because there are no lucrative worldwide water vapour markets. No one is talking about curbing our water vapour emissions because frankly the movers and business shakers of this world have not yet figured out a way to make money from water vapour emissions! So all of the attention is diverted to carbon dioxide as this is where the big bucks lie.

The present day levels of carbon dioxide are not even that high in a paleoclimatic context. I can see some readers throwing their arms in the air aghast at this statement. However our present levels of atmospheric carbon dioxide are still substantially lower than in previous geologic eras such as the Ordovician- Silurian epoch when carbon dioxide was 4000ppm.

During the Jurassic-Cretaceous epoch carbon dioxide levels were at 2000ppm. Interestingly there was glaciation during the Ordovician epoch despite very high levels of carbon dioxide. However this is a very complex issue that would take an entire book to discuss and explore. One of the reasons for such discrepancies in CO_2 levels and climate in our paleoclimatic record is to do with rock formation.

When the tectonic plates collided to form the Tibetan plateau and Himalayas the very high mountain range caused a drop in carbon dioxide levels as rocks weather and remove CO_2. Therefore levels fell after this mountain range rose up. The fluctuations of carbon dioxide can be affected greatly by such carbon sinks as rocks and soil.

If mankind is genuinely concerned about carbon dioxide levels they would curtail building and concreting over soil which is part of the carbon cycle.

However the main problem is undoubtedly pollution and not carbon dioxide.

Pollution will be our undoing as our seas become choked with plastic microbeads from our facial scrubs and cosmetic products. These days up to one third of caught fish now contain minute plastic microbeads that have found their way into the oceans down our drains. A healthy food source of omega essential fatty acids is now becoming clogged with toxic plastic.

This pollution of our planet is where our attention should be directed. We are slowly poisoning ourselves with toxins that are now routinely found in food samples. Livestock are pumped full of antibiotics and crops are sprayed with poisons. Yet attention has been diverted to global warming, as this is where the big money lies!

A problem with the carbon dioxide warming models is that while carbon dioxide may help to warm the troposphere it seems to have the opposite effect in the stratosphere. The stratosphere is a layer of the atmosphere that is 9 to 14 miles high above the Earth. The stratosphere is also where our protective ozone layer resides.

High up in the stratosphere carbon dioxide actually acts as a cooling agent. So carbon dioxide works in opposite ways in the stratosphere and the troposphere. We are all familiar with dry ice which is a freezing form of carbon dioxide.

It is possible that carbon dioxide has been overstated as a warming agent by the computer models. However when it comes to climate studies some of the best and faultless data comes from the geologic record.

There can be no disputing what has already occurred on our planet! This geologic record shows that for the past 2 million years there have been major ice ages lasting around 100, 000 years punctuated by interglacials lasting approximately 10, 000 years. We are now at the 11, 750 year mark in our interglacial, the Holocene, and hence our major ice age is possibly overdue.

The Mayan Long Count calendar predicted an end of a planetary era in 2012. Although I tend to be driven by hard logic and facts, a thought fleetingly crossed my mind that this major event might be referring to a new ice age. Such an event would most certainly mark the end of an old era and the beginning of a new epoch as the Long Count predicted. Intuition tells me that we are at the dawn of a new age, and this new epoch is the expected ice age!

As the late Sir Fred Hoyle rightly pointed out, the main reason our atmosphere traps heat is water vapour and the hydrosphere. If the water vapour were to turn into minute ice crystals over the Northern Hemisphere we would have an instant ice age as the shiny ice crystals would exert a strong light reflecting albedo effect. Water vapour makes a wonderful greenhouse gas until it turns to ice!

Yet scientists are still researching ways to geo-engineer and cool our planet. A very minute layer of reflective particles around our atmosphere could precipitate an instant ice age as the late Sir Fred Hoyle wrote in his book called "Ice". In this book written in 1979 he describes how a very thin dust veil around the globe made from iced water vapour crystals or space dust would take a mere six months to initiate a full blown ice age!

Hence one can see just how very dangerous the proposal to geo-engineer our climate with minute aerosol particles would be. An irreversible ice age could start that would be self sustaining. Once the ice and snow of the ice age has arrived it would become self reinforcing because of the white ice reflective albedo effect.

As the Earth grows colder from the geo-engineered particles another feedback loop would kick in. As temperatures plummet the warming water vapour in our atmosphere would start to freeze into minute ice crystals. These sparkling ice crystals would shine like a transparent veil of diamond dust. The frozen crystals would then reflect even more of the sun`s radiation back into space thus beckoning a cataclysmic ice age.

Even if the geo-engineered particles were to eventually fall back to Earth the resultant ice crystals that formed would continue to sustain a most terrible ice age. It would be bitterly ironic if mankind succeeded in geoengineering a new ice age when one is already arriving soon! It is possible that covert experiments are already taking place to cool our planet; in which case we can expect the mother of all ice ages!

Chapter 8: Polar Vortex, Arctic Amplification and Jet Streams.

We are all aware of just how unreliable our weather forecasts can be. I vividly recall the evening in 1987 when weather forecaster Michael Fish announced that a lady had phoned in to say that there was a hurricane on the way. He assured the television audience that there was no need to worry and that there was absolutely not a chance of a hurricane sweeping across the British Isles. Later that night I was woken by a ferocious howling noise of wind screeching through the gap in my window.

I peeked out through the curtains and noticed that a neighbouring silver birch tree that usually stood tall and straight was now completely bent at a right angle and the top was almost touching the ground! I had never seen a tree at such a strange angle before and it looked like it had bent in half. I then fell asleep and slept peacefully through one of the worst hurricanes to batter our shores. The nation awoke to scenes of chaos the following morning. This taught me a salutary lesson about the reliability weather forecasts!

Still there can be no doubt that the weather in the British Isles is greatly influenced by cold air masses such as the polar vortex and by the jet stream. The polar vortex and the jet stream work together in a synergistic fashion bringing weather systems to Great

Britain. Therefore a discussion of the polar vortex and the jet stream is combined in this chapter.

The mass of cold air that hovers over our poles is known as a polar vortex. This term became a popular media buzzword during the recent freezing winters in North America and the U.K. When polar arctic air descends we have glacial conditions. Conversely when the milder westerly winds blow the weather is warmer and wetter during the winter months.

During our recent snowy winters, weather forecasters and meteorologists spoke of a freezing polar vortex that had become stuck for a lengthy period bringing exceptionally biting cold temperatures. There are actually two polar vortices. The stratospheric polar vortex is 19,800 metres (**65,000 feet**) above the surface of the Earth.

The tropospheric polar vortex is around 5,500 to 9,100 metres (**18,000 to 30,000 feet**) above the surface. Usually, when the weather forecasters are talking about the polar vortex, they're referring to the tropospheric vortex. Remember that the lower troposphere is the layer of the atmosphere where most of our weather patterns arise.

A polar vortex air mass is influenced by the position of the northern jet stream. The fast moving air flow known as the Jet stream can change direction from an East/West direction to a North/South direction over Great Britain. This enables the freezing polar air mass to descend over the British

Isles. In the UK, extreme conditions were experienced in the winter of 2010.

The normal pattern of Arctic winds broke down causing a polar vortex to allow a frigid body of air to move south. This brought record snow conditions to northern Europe, eastern Asia and eastern North America and to Great Britain. According to the Office for National Statistics, there were nearly 44,000 excess winter deaths in the cold winter of 2014-15.
A particularly cold winter puts elderly and vulnerable people at risk. There are heating problems as boilers breakdown and roads become dangerous.

The polar vortex descended over the British Isles in January 2017 bringing freezing conditions. Some scientists such as Timo Vihma from the Finnish

Meteorological Institute are hypothesising that the polar vortex is weakening over the Arctic due to a loss of sea ice. **The question is being asked if the warming of the Arctic could cause the jet stream to meander and to wander south.** When the polar vortex is strong it remains firmly in place over the North Pole.

When it weakens it descends bringing the polar air mass over the Northern hemisphere. However if melting arctic ice is the cause of the weakening polar vortex this would not explain why it does not always descend as in the mild winter of 2015. There may be other causes of aberrations in the polar vortex. The polar vortex may possibly be responding more to changes in the northerly jet stream instead of to melting Arctic ice.

Another theory proposes that the jet stream is becoming more undulating instead of remaining in a smooth tight circle above the Arctic. When the jet stream loops down it drags the cold air with it. So the whole of Great Britain is then covered in a freezing polar air mass that normally would sit tight in the Arctic Circle. The jet stream is therefore becoming more kinked and wavy instead of remaining in a tight circular motion.

Jet streams are very fast moving air streams that are generated by the Coriolis force from the rotation of the Earth. The Coriolis force is caused by the rotation of earth on its axis. Jet streams are also affected by differences in temperature gradients from North to South. The jet stream in turn is affected by changes in solar activity. This is a very complex area worthy of research by an atmospheric physicist. Perhaps this phenomenon could be used as evidence that a global warming could lead to a cooling?

There is a phenomenon known as a sudden stratospheric warming which can affect the polar vortex in way that gives rise to colder temperatures for Great Britain. It may seem like a contradiction in terms to learn that a sudden warning of this very high stratospheric layer can result in cooling below. A Sudden Stratospheric Warming (SSW) event occurs when there is an abrupt warming of air, which is introduced into the cold Arctic polar vortex.

The reasons behind this are complex and the results are dramatic. An SSW event results when the cold arctic air mass gets pushed due south. The freezing cold air is carried south by the jet stream. An SSW cold weather event was responsible for freezing weeks of weather in Scotland in February 2018. This may seem confusing, so in a nutshell, a Sudden Stratospheric Warming event means freezing weather for Great Britain.

The stratospheric polar vortex can completely disintegrate and cause a wind flow pattern to reverse in the opposite direction. This can have an amplified effect on weather patterns in the troposphere which is the atmospheric layer found just beneath the stratosphere. An increase in blocking high patterns weather can inhibit the normal flow of the jet stream. When a weather system becomes blocked it remains stationary.

These disruptive patterns can last up to two months and cold Arctic weather can be experienced at latitudes further south.

Conversely when the stratosphere is colder it leads to a stronger jet stream that locks the cold polar air mass safely over the Arctic.

So a cold stratosphere can keep Great Britain bathed in a warmer jet stream air flow. While a SSW event makes Great Britain much colder. So paradoxically a sudden Stratospheric Warming Event causes a polar vortex air flow due to a kink in our jet stream.

The stratospheric warming leads to our westerly winds being suppressed and since the mild westerlies warm the British Isles this leads to a cooler air flow. When the wind comes from the east we have the "beast of the East" Siberian winds blowing. So there are two cold air patterns affecting the climate in Great Britain which are the north and the east winds. Conversely the west and southerly winds bring milder air flows.

Seemingly anomalous stratospheric warming effects indicate the complexities of atmospheric physics. A stratospheric warming can also cause the jet stream to reverse bringing cold eastern Siberian winds to the U.K. It is thought by scientists such as Mike Lockwood that such a cold easterly wind pattern may have prevailed during the last mini ice age.

March 1st 2018 saw the Siberian east wind bring biting cold and record amounts of snow. Indeed the cold east wind dominated the entire month and spring was late in arriving here in the British Isles. America suffered a similar fate and snow fell on April 1st in Washington DC, Philadelphia and Minnesota. These colder north east wind patterns will prevail when the ice age arrives in force.

Stratospheric warming events occur when large atmospheric waves, known as Rossby waves, extend beyond the troposphere where most of our usual weather occurs, and into the stratosphere.

This vertical transport of energy can set a complex process into motion that leads to the breakdown of the high altitude cold low pressure area that typically spins above the North Pole during the winter. This is leads to the polar vortex flow. **These undulating** waves were first identified in the Earth's atmosphere in 1939 by Carl-Gustaf Arvid Rossby who went on to explain their motion.

When the Rossby waves hit the stratosphere the polar vortex is disrupted. What is a Rossby wave exactly? These waves are large ripples found in both oceans and atmosphere. A Rossby wave may consist of a high pressure ridge that is blocked from moving or disintegrating. They appear to be caused by the rotation of the Earth. This rotation is also known as the Coriolis force.

Rossby waves owe their origin to the tangential speed of the planetary rotation. This is a complex mathematical topic so I am keeping it very simple.Some scientists believe that the Rossby waves may be responsible for some of our extreme long lasting weather events recorded in the Northern Hemisphere. These stationary weather events have been characterised by a blocking high or anticyclones that have become stuck in one position for a long time. For example when there is a very long period of warmth as in the famous summer of 2003 this is due to a blocking high anticyclone weather pattern.

A similar stationary blocking high can cause a huge mass of cold air to stagnate for weeks bringing weeks of cold weather and ice. The weather front has in effect become blocked from moving and disintegrating so to speak and so remains stagnant. A blocking high pressure system or anticyclone can cause smogs if the air hangs over a polluted city for a long time.

A winter anticyclone can be clear and frosty or perhaps foggy and the air is still without any wind. A summer anticyclone can bring an endless succession of blue sky and sunshine filled days. Think of the unusually sunny and warm British summers of 1976 and 2003 to get an idea of how a blocked anticyclone weather pattern will cause a prolonged spell of weather.

Some meteorologists think that extreme weather events such as the widespread flooding event in Europe in 2013 and the 2012 China flooding are caused by a resonant amplification of Earth`s Rossby waves (Petoukhov, Ramstorf et al 2013). The following abstract of the Rossby wave paper states that,

"In recent years, the Northern Hemisphere has suffered several devastating regional summer weather extremes, such as the European heat wave in 2003, the Russian heat wave, the Indus river flood in Pakistan in 2010, and the United States heat wave in 2011. We propose a common mechanism for the generation of persistent longitudinal planetary-scale high-amplitude patterns of the atmospheric circulation in the Northern Hemisphere mid latitudes. Zonal wave numbers, m = 6, 7, or 8 are characteristic of the above weather extremes."

I have copied the transcript word for word so as to give an accurate representation of the theory. As one can see there is no mention of rising carbon dioxide levels to explain these extreme weather events. The events appear to be due to Earth`s rotational Coriolis effect and solar activity rather than to an anthropogenic warming caused by our carbon dioxide emissions. These days every single unusual weather event is blamed on carbon dioxide or greenhouse gases and this is rather naïve.

In the Northern Hemisphere the anticyclone rotates clockwise around the globe. In the Southern Hemisphere it rotates anti-clockwise. As mentioned previously these rotations are caused by the Coriolis effect of Earth`s rotation. These atmospheric waves are also responsible for dust storms in America. The British Met Office said that one type of jet stream factor known to affect weather is the quasi-biennial oscillation (QBO).

This cycle, discovered in 1959, involves a narrow band of fast moving winds like the jet stream which sits about 15 miles up over the equator. Waves known as gravity waves give rise to the Quasi Biennial Oscillation or QBO wind pattern.

The QBO is believed to affect the ozone layer in the stratosphere. Eastward phases of the QBO often coincide with a sudden stratospheric warming and cold winters in northern Europe and eastern USA. Westward phases of the QBO coincide with mild winters in eastern USA.

The QBO correlates with a strong Atlantic jet stream. This brings mild and wet stormy winters to northern Europe and the British Isles. Such a wild wet weather system affected the British Isles in 2012.During the Queen`s diamond jubilee in the summer month of June, it rained so much that six people were taken to a London hospital with hypothermia!

The rains continued unabated for days and holiday campers had to be evacuated from flooded caravan parks in Wales. By September over 570 homes had been flooded according to the Environment Agency. The heavy rains and flooding continued until late November 2012 causing extensive damage and a lot of heartbreak as people surveyed their flooded homes. Some houses even collapsed and were washed into gushing rivers nearby.

During early spring 2012 the UK was positioned under a strong high pressure region resulting in very dry and warm conditions which brought a mini heat wave. Then everything changed in

April, when the wave pattern underwent a significant shift. This shift put the British Isles at the mercy of strong low pressure weather systems. This low system brought relentless torrents of rain from the prevailing south-westerly flow and rivers burst their banks and bridges collapsed.

Motorists became trapped in their cars as the waters suddenly rose and a man died under a bridge. This relentless flooding was blamed on the jet stream by the Met Office. The wet weather was partly due to an aberration of the Rossby wave pattern according to meteorologists. The jet stream became disturbed in the Northern Hemisphere. This disturbance then resulted in **a Rossby wave** pattern of both high and low pressure regions.

The projected climate models for a global warming predict that our summers will become hotter and drier and grape vineyards would soon be flourishing here! However a lot of our weather here in Great Britain is at the mercy of the prevailing pattern of jet streams. These in turn are influenced by planetary Rossby waves.

An eastward phase coincides with a weaker Atlantic jet stream and cold winters in Northern Europe and eastern USA whereas westward phases of the QBO often coincide with mild winters in eastern USA and a strong Atlantic jet stream with mild, wet stormy winters in northern Europe. In addition, the QBO has been shown to affect hurricane frequency during hurricane seasons in the Atlantic.

Research has also been conducted investigating a possible relationship between ENSO (El Nino Southern Oscillation) and the QBO. Will any loss of sea ice influence the Rossby wave pattern?

Has the planetary Rossby wave activity changed in recent decades and is it likely to do so under a projected future warming? If it is changing, is the rapid Arctic warming indeed responsible? Is there a relation with climate change and Rossby wave patterns? These are some of the questions that are being asked by climate scientists James Screen and Ian Simmonds.

The Phenomenon known as Arctic amplification leads to a greater warming then anticipated at the Poles. As the Arctic warms it displaces cold air that then drops down over the British Isles. Arctic amplification refers to a far greater amount of warmth than should be expected from the actual amount of heat that has been convected from equatorial regions.

This phenomenon of the Arctic climate has been thoroughly researched by the distinguished and highly accomplished American oceanographer Dr. James Overland. It is akin to the famous butterfly effect chaos theory proposed by Edward Lorenz whereby a small change in an initial parameter can lead to a much large effect than anticipated.

Arctic amplification may also cause kinks in the path of the jet stream leading it to drop down instead of remaining as a tight circular belt around the North Pole. An increasing trend of cold Arctic air dropping over America and the British Isles is projected to increase in the future leading to bitterly cold winters. A team based at Sheffield University confirms that Arctic warming may affect the position of the jet stream resulting in cold winters across America and Northern Europe.

Many extreme weather events are actually correlated with jet stream activity and are not the result of carbon emissions. There is also a phenomenon known as Arctic amplification. This is the term given to the fact that a change in heat radiation will tend to result in an amplified change in temperature near the Arctic. So the warming at the Arctic or Antarctic will be far greater than that of the average temperature.

Rutgers University climate scientist Jennifer Francis and colleagues link a wavy jet stream to a warming Arctic. The team believes that climate changes near the top of the world are happening faster than in Earth's middle latitudes. Prof Jennifer Francis of Rutgers University in the US said that "This heavy rainfall does seem to suggest that weather patterns are changing and people are noticing that the weather in their area is not what it used to be".

Recently the atmospheric jet stream which transports weather systems has taken to meandering all over North America. This has resulted in prolonged cold snaps on the East Coast. Wavy jet stream patterns have been occurring frequently since the 1990s, and are now affecting weather around the Northern Hemisphere.

Jennifer Francis is Professor at the Institute of Marine and Coastal Sciences at Rutgers University. She thinks that the new Arctic amplification warming pattern is causing extreme weather in America such as droughts and heavy snow fall.

Exceptionally cold winters are being reinforced by a meandering jet stream dragging down a cold polar vortex. This has caused some record snowfalls in America recently. The phenomenon known as Arctic amplification is caused by disproportionate Arctic warming that in turn is causing the Northern Hemisphere circulation to assume a more meridional wavy character. This phenomenon of Arctic amplification might be causing highly amplified jet-stream patterns bringing freakish weather events (Francis & Skific 2015).

These strange events could actually be a sign of an ice age onset as there is evidence of similar Arctic warming before the end of the last interglacial known as the end Eemian. During an ice age the Arctic may paradoxically become warmer while the northern land masses become laden with snow and ice. There were large settlements of Inuit populations in the Arctic from the time of the last ice age, and the transit of people into North America could support this warmer Arctic hypothesis.

Most of Alaska was ice free during the last Ice Age and connected to Siberia by the now submerged land bridge called Beringia (Smith 2000). Early people migrated from Siberia to America across this land bridge. Interestingly to this day there is a strong facial resemblance between the ethnic communities of Alaska and Siberia.

Meridional jet streams can divert warm air into Arctic regions. In this way natural climate change gives us colder mid latitudes with more snow and ice cover during ice ages but strangely there may be warmer temperatures at the poles!

It appears that the ice is somehow displaced and ends up covering Northern America and the United Kingdom. During interglacials we see warmer mid latitudes with less snow and ice cover and colder poles. Therefore the fact that the Arctic seems to be warming now could be a clear warning sign that a new ice age is arriving soon in the Northern hemisphere.

The reader may recall that the temperature on the graphs peak just before a rapid descent into an ice age. Recent warm decades provide the sort of data that one would expect to see just before the arrival of an ice age. Even the much publicised warming of the Arctic regions ties in with a predicted ice age event. In other words it always gets much warmer just before it gets cooler!

Conversely during interglacials we see warmer mid latitudes with less snow and ice cover and colder poles! So one can see that the scenario of an ice age is not entirely straight forward! Therefore the fact that the Arctic seems to be warming now could be a clear warning sign that a new ice age is arriving soon in the Northern Hemisphere!

Politicians of all political Parties have been milking anthropogenic climate change for all its worth. Climate change has provided an ideal excuse for their incompetence regarding the recent floods in Great Britain. During Storm Desmond over 16,000 homes were flooded. In December 2015 the Army evacuated 2000 residents from their homes and the Lake District was severely flooded in 2015. Many cases of homes flooding could have been prevented by proper Government investment in flood barriers and were probably avoidable. In 2014 the UK experienced a spell of extreme wet weather from late January to February as a succession of major storms brought widespread damage to the UK.

In December 2015 Leeds council leader Judith Blake accused the

Government of discriminating between north and south when it comes to flood defence spending, saying that residents in her city were not getting "anywhere near the support that we saw going into Somerset" last year. Somerset used to flood regularly in centuries gone by.

Indeed the name Somerset derives from the word summer lands since Somerset was considered in days gone by to be only habitable during summer! This pattern of heavy rain fall was prevalent during the last Little Ice Age also. As the rains bore down on Somerset the Somerset levels became an island and residents were cut off by a moat! I suggested that our government make an application for assistance from the EU Disaster Fund.

The Government then proceeded to use climate change as a political comfort blanket to abrogate itself from any blame and incompetency. It was mischievously alleged that Lord Smith who was the Minister for The Environment had spent as much money on wining and dining in fine hotels as he had on dredging the rivers which had burst their banks! The departing environment Minister Lord Smith was feeling rather upset and so he decided to be cross with the hapless Lord Owen Paterson for not investing more money to adapt to climate change.

Accusing fingers were being pointed in all directions! An endless stream of Government Ministers such as Philip Hammond appeared on the news blaming the floods on climate change instead of a lack of Government investment in flood defences and infrastructure. It was all because of an act of God and that villain, carbon dioxide, that the rivers had burst their banks.

The blame was shrewdly shifted on invisible gases rather than the Ministers own incompetency. "Phew! This idea of climate change is proving remarkably useful chaps!" Now global warming could be held accountable for the endless mistakes and negligence of the ruling politicians. Now each and every flood caused by a lack of investment in maintaining rivers and flood barriers, could be blamed on the new fall guy, Mr. climate change!

The Met Office tried in vain to explain that the flooding had been due to the jet stream and that the jet stream is not affected in any way by greenhouse gases. However most of the time they simply went with the flow and tide of public opinion and said what the politicians wanted them to say.

"Yes indeed we can expect to see more of this flooding as the climate changes in the coming future" the weather forecasters would say as they pointed to the flooded areas on the map of the British Isles. Of course this shifts the locus of responsibility away from the politicians who are running our country and gets them neatly off the hook.

This is a prize winning picture of Cornwall taken by Bernie Pettersen during the storms in February 2014

The photo above won first prize in a competition run by the aptly named Shipwrecked Mariners Society! Still as the floods and storms raged at the back of everyone's mind lurked the question "is this the beginning of the end for humanity as climate change wreaks havoc on our shores?"

We have two wind patterns that are associated with bitterly cold weather in the U.K. and these are northerly and easterly winds. In contrast our southerly and westerly winds tend to bring warmer and milder weather. In England, prevailing west winds bring rain from the Atlantic. In winter, an east wind blowing from Northern

Europe is always cold and often brings sleet and snow.

Following a sudden stratospheric warming, the high altitude winds reverse to flow eastward instead of their usual westward. The eastward winds progress down through the atmosphere and weaken the jet stream, often giving easterly winds near the surface and resulting in dramatic reductions in temperature in Europe.

It is thought that during the Maunder Minimum brought about by low sunspot activity, there was a coincidental change in wind direction induced by the jet stream. So the British Isles had a continual cold air stream coming over from Russia in an easterly air flow which caused temperatures to plummet like a hail stone. So somehow there may be a connection between low sunspot activity and a change in our prevailing winter winds that serve to reinforce each other.

A recent paper was published in Nature Geoscience showing how low solar activity is correlated to jet stream blocking events. The authors looked at data going back for one thousand years for solar activity and climate. The study found a correlation between low sunspot solar activity and an increase in winter blocking anticyclone systems.

The team think that to the west of the British Isles there was a stubborn mass of air that blocked the warm westerly winds. This blocking high pressure system was being driven by the low solar activity. The researchers found that this anticyclone not only prevented the mild westerly air flow but it encouraged the colder air to dropdown from the North and East. This air pattern was behind the freezing winters of late in the British Isles (Nature Geoscience 2014).

This is the prevailing weather pattern that caused our country to become so very cold during the winters of the Maunder Minimum era of very low sunspots.

Other meteorological studies have also confirmed that there is a relationship between solar variability and winter anticyclones and it is thought to be caused via the stratosphere. The lead author of the study in Cardiff University found a correlation with both the ocean and atmospheric dynamics during low sunspot activity.

The Welsh Cardiff University study was conducted in collaboration with the University of Bern. The team found that solar activity influenced the ocean-atmosphere dynamics in the North Atlantic Sea.

This would lead to a vast effect on regional climate as the Gulf Stream would be affected. Professor Ian Hall said that they had used sediments taken from the seafloor in Iceland. The data was used to reconstruct both temperature and salinity of the seawater for the past 1000 years.

The study found that there were large temperature changes over time and that colder and less salty water was correlated with low solar activity. Professor Ian Hall was a co author of the study and he said that "By using the climate model it was also possible to explore how the changes in solar output affected the surface circulation of the Atlantic Ocean". "The circulation of the surface of the Atlantic Ocean is typically tightly linked to changes in the wind patterns". (Moffa-Sanchez et al 2014).

I find this research very interesting as it coincides neatly with recent findings by Bill Turrell on the Faroe Islands in Scotland about our Gulf Stream waters. Turrell noted that the salinity of the Gulf Stream is decreasing faster than at any time previously recorded. He is worried that it means our Gulf Stream is slowing down and may even stop altogether which would drastically affect our climate. I do not think that he has linked his findings with those of the solar physicists, and yet there is clearly a connection.

The academic focus has been directed on carbon dioxide emissions. Consequently this obvious connection between solar activity and our North Atlantic Ocean currents and Gulf Stream is being overlooked. It looks like the British Isles could soon be in a lot of trouble if the predicted low solar activity arrives in 2025.

Solar physicists have also been recording a steady fall in the solar wind that will continue to decline until the Sun goes into hibernation so to speak during the solar cycles 25 to 26.

This solar decline in turn could affect our Gulf Stream which is part of the North Atlantic Oscillation (NAO). A diminution of the solar wind could theoretically cause the Gulf Stream to slow down or stop completely.

The North Atlantic Oscillation is a weather phenomenon in the North Atlantic involving atmospheric pressures at the sea level. The oscillation varies as a result of Icelandic lows and highs from the Azores down south. These differentials create oscillations and the effects are felt here in the British Isles as the westerly winds and currents can vary. The NAO is also part of the Arctic oscillation ocean current.

The winter of 2009–10 in Europe was unusually cold. It is hypothesized that this may be due to a combination of low solar activity and the jet streams (Science Daily 2010).

The memorably snowy winter of 2010 was also observed to have a strong Easterly phase of the Quasi-Biennial Oscillation.

This low solar activity resulted in the British Isles looking as if it had descended into an ice age. The satellite photograph below shows the exact amount of snow and ice cover that we would expect to see over the British Isles permanently during a new ice age.

The Met Office reported that the UK, had experienced its coldest winter for 30 years in 2009/2010 and again the coldest March day occurred in 2018. This cold also coincided with an exceptionally negative phase of the North Atlantic Oscillation. Thus we can see how low solar activity can affect the North Atlantic Oscillation and other ocean currents to bring very cold winter weather to the British Isles.

Some of our memorably wet winters were caused by jet stream anomalies and not carbon emissions please note!

Jet streams are in turn caused by a combination of a planet's rotation on its axis and atmospheric heating by solar radiation. The jet stream is a band of fast moving westerly winds high up in the atmosphere which circle around the pole in the Northern Hemisphere. It can feature winds of up to 200 knots or more.

A strong westerly jet stream can bring wet and windy weather systems off the Atlantic and even cause flooding. The jet stream moves around and its position can have a big impact on weather here in the UK depending on where it is. If the jet is over the UK or just to the south, we tend to get a lot of wet and windy conditions as it brings weather systems straight to us.

If the jet is to the north of us, it guides that changeable weather away to the north to leave the UK with more settled conditions. In centuries past cottages had reed matting on floors. When the floods came you moved all possessions upstairs and the matting could be discarded and replaced.

Great Britain may lose a tremendous amount of warmth when the winds change direction and the Gulf Stream slows. We will need more energy and this concerns me a great deal. If the solar physicists are correct then we should soon see a pattern of very cold icy winters starting to kick in. Biting cold north easterly wind patterns will prevail and we will need all the power and energy possible to keep ourselves warm.

As a small island we are at the mercy of prevailing wind and ocean currents. The Gulf Stream brings us free heat equivalent to a million power stations. If our sun goes to sleep, both the warm westerlies winds and the Gulf Stream will switch off. Therefore if solar activity switches both of these heat sources away from our vulnerable Isles, it is easy to comprehend how a little ice age will occur. The riddle of our climatic variables has been solved and it seems that we are in a precarious position.

 The question dangling in the air like a shivering icicle is what will happen to the benign climate of the British Isles? There is no certainty but a sense of foreboding looms. We are in a vulnerable position. The problem is that Great Britain lies much farther north than most people realise.

 The odds are all tipping us towards another ice age. While we feel safely cuckooned in our comfy bubble that is heated by the Gulf Stream and mild westerlies, an ice age looms. A prolonged kink in our jet stream may bring us cold east winds or an Arctic blast that one day may precipitate our ice age. If I was a gambler my bet would be that the future of the British Isles is not one of fragrant vineyards but one that is covered in ice!

Chapter 9: Energy Security for a Colder Climate

Great Britain is now a world leader when it comes to saving energy! Amazingly our frugal island is now using less energy per capita than was used in the swinging sixties! This is even more impressive when one considers that there has been an increase in population.

An analysis has shown that this lower consumption is due to new insulation measures and innovative energy saving appliances. There has been a technological explosion of energy saving gadgets such as low energy kettles, though some consumers complain that they take too long to boil!

The idea that using more energy will lead to a runaway global warming has had a useful result for the Government. Consumers are now terrified that if they leave a light on it will have dire repercussions on the climate. The Climate Change Bill was introduced in Parliament in 2007. The Bill contained provisions that set a legally binding target for reducing U.K. carbon dioxide emissions by at least 26% by 2020 and 60% by 2050 compared to baseline 1990 levels. The Bill stipulated that the Government publish five yearly carbon budget reports.

A Committee on Climate Change has also been created. The Act requires the Committee to advise the Government on the levels of carbon budget to be set. It stipulates that there is a balance between domestic emissions and the use of carbon credits and intends that the 2050 emissions target is increased to greater levels. The Act has a commercial angle and provides powers to establish trading schemes for the purpose of limiting greenhouse gas.

This innovative Bill became law on 26 November 2008 as the Climate Change

Act. This seminal and ground-breaking piece of legislation was the world's first ever legally binding framework to tackle the dangers of climate change that is presumed to have an anthropogenic basis.

As a result of this legislation there is currently a predicted energy deficit of around 10-16 GW due to our 15 coal power station closures. Recently demand for energy is falling due to energy saving appliances and at the moment the threat of power cuts is receding. A lot of energy is being saved due to microgeneration of energy by individual homeowners via solar panels and small turbines.

The EU Large Combustion Plant Directive has also made the problem of our energy security even worse as it stipulates that our working power stations must be closed. This deficit may lead to power cuts if energy savings are not made. Fortunately in Great Britain we now use less energy than was used in the swinging sixties, when Carnaby Street fashion and flower power reigned supreme. However we are paying higher electricity bills, despite using less energy and some may feel that this is a tad unfair on the consumer.

It would have been wiser for our government to have planted millions of trees instead of closing our vital power stations. Coal power stations have been converted to burn wood pellets instead. This ridiculous idea is known as biomass which sounds almost as if it might actually be good for the environment. Of course felling acres of woods to use as fuel is a highly regressive step. Much of the wood is imported from pristine forests in America. Large areas of forest are being cleared to provide wood pellets for Drax power station, in the misguided belief that wood is somehow better than coal as a fuel.

  There is no doubt that human beings are leaving an indelible and pernicious footprint on our planet Earth. It is right that legal frameworks are being enacted in order to attempt to curb this deleterious impact. However the sheer logistics of trying to implement legal cuts in carbon need to be examined in the light of the fact that all life on our planet is carbon based and we eat carbohydrates every day! The security of our long term energy is of serious concern as our economy depends on reliable and cheap energy in order to flourish.

There is great concern that a looming energy gap may arise that cripple industry in a disturbing echo of the 1970`s strikes that culminated in the 1979 "Winter of Discontent". Mature readers may remember the crippling waves of strikes and power cuts in the decade of the 1970`s. In December 1970 hospitals had to work under candlelight during widespread work to rule strikes. The Conservative Prime Minister Ted Heath declared a three day working week since there was not enough electricity to make it worth going to work after a wave of angry miners` and union backed strikes.

The reserves of coal needed for electricity generation were running low and so a three day week was mandatory to conserve what little power remained. The price of oil was also at a record high due to factors in the Middle East and so Britain had to rely on its own coal. The Prime Minister called on the nation to curtail their power use and television was shut off early each night. Even floodlights were banned at evening outdoor sporting events so they rescheduled matches for the day time.

   There was a sense of a wartime blitz community spirit as candlelight uncooked cold dinners became the norm in blackout Britain. In 1973 Slade`s hit merry Christmas got to number one and people were determined to enjoy the festive season despite the power cuts!

   The short working week miraculously did not have a crippling effect on industry but the economy was not as productive. The generating power supply was precarious and power would be cut without warning. The country was in chaos and rubbish piled high in the streets and rats ran rife.

Then Edward Heath lost the election in 1974 to Harold Wilson. If the public hoped for an improvement they would be in for a disappointment. The newly elected Labour Government then also upset the trade unions by reneging on their contracts with the TUC (Trades Union Council) over pay caps.

There were strikes at Ford motors and unrest spread like wildfire across the country. The unions were effectively holding the Government to ransom. The turbulent decade of the seventies, filled with wonderful pop and rock anthems, culminated in the memorable winter of 1979. This was known as the Winter of Discontent in a parody of the famous opening words spoken in Shakespeare`s play, King Richard.

The coldest winter for years coincided with militant strikes by lorry drivers and public sector employees. The electorate was weary, and in 1979 they returned Conservative Margaret Thatcher known as the iron lady to restore order once more. This steely lady was not for turning, and she would not give in to militant miners who were justifiably striking for better pay and working conditions. The British Government was having a lot of trouble with its coal mines at the time and violent clashes were taking place between the police and the miners.

The indomitable Prime Minister therefore devised a cunning plan to deal with the problem of striking miners and coal shortages. The plan was to demonise coal in order to promote nuclear power. Nuclear would become the main energy provider for blackout Britain. This ingenious plan would then justify the closure of the coal mines which would be replaced by new nuclear power stations. To justify such a radical plan the shrewd politician decided to give a compelling speech on the dangers of burning fossil fuels for energy.

She enlisted the help of her Chief Scientific Adviser, Crispin Tickell to write her groundbreaking speech before the United Nations General Assembly. Crispin Tickell was an expert on the latest scientific theories about fossil fuels. At that time some scientists feared that burning fossil fuels could harm the environment, although there was no consensus as to whether burning coal might heat the planet. Some scientists felt it would lead to as cooling. The topic of carbon dioxide and fossil fuels had previously been a rather niche and obscure theory that was relegated to the archives of oblivion.

Suddenly this obscure scientific hypothesis about coal and fossil fuels was in the limelight and given full publicity in the year of 1989. The speech aimed to demonise coal power as being bad for the planet. The speech about global warming and fossil fuels written by her Chief Scientific Adviser made a great impression at the United Nations Assembly. The speech made the Prime Minister seem intellectual with a brilliant grasp of science! This seminal speech about the dangers of burning fossil fuels would hopefully pave the way for a generation of new nuclear power stations and put an end to the troublesome miners` strikes.

However at some point the Chancellor of the Exchequer at the time made an observation. This Chancellor is the well known politician named Nigel Lawson. The shrew financier pointed out to the Iron Lady that nuclear power might prove to be prohibitively expensive to the public purse. Subsequently the policy of building more "low carbon" nuclear power stations was quietly shelved and the topic was once more laid to bed and all but forgotten about. Once politicians abandon an idea it tends to once more become an obscure scientific theory!

Perhaps the astute Conservative Party Chancellor Nigel Lawson also had his hidden doubts about the mixing of niche scientific theories together with major political policy? Intriguingly Nigel Lawson now chairs a think tank called the Global Warming Policy Foundation. This charity aims to bring clarity to the debate of anthropogenic warming. I find this somewhat amusing and tend to think that his cynicism about fossil fuels may have had something to do with the speech written that helped to justify the closure of our coal mines. Mixing politics with science tends to arouse suspicion in an enquiring mind. However Nigel Lawson is far too polite and loyal to ever mention his doubts about the speech on carbon dioxide and global warming made by the formidable Iron Lady!

The idea to close down the mines and coal power stations was shelved until it was resurrected in the 1990`s. At some point green leaning politicians may have called on the expertise of the former chief scientific adviser`s son Oliver Tickell who lives in Oxford to explain the greenhouse effect and his Father`s speech. The Green Politician Caroline Lucas began her successful career in Oxford. There can be no doubt that she is a most gifted and articulate politician. With her eloquent skills she persuaded many EU members that the time had come to eschew coal power.

A sudden surge of campaigning and protests organised at coal power stations orchestrated by the nascent Green Party. It seemed that the idea was suddenly very fashionable as a protest. One felt that they had adopted this anti coal policy rather hastily and that it may have had something to do with the Iron Lady`s speech, that popularised the idea of fossil fuels leading to global warming.

Numerous protests started taking place at power stations. Caroline Lucas a Green Party MP held colourful and enjoyable climate camps at Kingsnorth Power Station. This camp proved very popular with environmentalists who were becoming increasingly convinced that the power station would lead to global warming. A lot of fun was had at the climate camps and some good environmental ideas were promoted such as micro generation of electricity with small solar panels.

However these endless protests at power stations must have started to grate on the Labour Government. At Kingsnorth Power Station protesters had climbed up to the top and draped a banner over it saying "Gordon". This name was referring to the Prime Minister at the time Gordon Brown for the Labour Party. The banner was clearly a tactic by the Green Party to win votes from the Labour Party at the time. The inference was that the Labour Party and Gordon Brown did not give a damn about the environment as they had not shut down the coal power stations!

The Green Party were perhaps hoping that their campaign and endless summer climate camps by the power station would win them some votes. The Labour Party was meanwhile incessantly vilified as being a Party that did not care about the climate and the environment. Meanwhile the more publicity that the climate protests were getting at the power stations the more money the newly formed band of carbon traders stood to make. Perhaps some of these carbon entrepreneurs were the master puppeteers covertly hiding in the back ground and quietly pulling the strings on their willing puppets?

Protests at coal power stations became more and more frequent. The climate actions were becoming dangerous since protesters were now scaling the high cooling towers! The Labour Government started to cave in and agreed that more must be done to prevent these power stations from operating.

Legislation started to be passed by the Labour government calling for curbs in carbon emissions from coal .This new legislation played right into the hands of the carbon entrepreneurs. Soon the lucrative carbon buckyball was rolling with unstoppable momentum. Carbon was now officially a poison and lucrative permits to pollute soon were being traded all over the world!

Whereas once coal was once king in the British Isles it had now become a dirty word. Industry powered by coal had made Great Britain the richest country in the world in the Edwardian era. Coal was glorified by railway steam engines such as the Flying Scotsman. Sadly the demise of coal meant that it would now serve to make a select few canny carbon traders rich by the fact its use had to be curtailed.

Suddenly all of the main political parties were keen to jump on this new anti fossil fuel bandwagon. Every political party was now proclaiming their climate credentials with each party vying to seem keener than the other party in a bid to win votes from the concerned public. Even the Conservative party leader David Cameron went to the Arctic on a photo shoot and declared that he would save the polar bears! Cameron urged voters to "vote blue to go green".

The reader can now see that the topic of coal has become a political football being passed around and used to win votes from a gullible electorate. Clearly this climate topic was seen as a massive vote winner and every politician soon began to profess a great concern for manmade climate change.

Anthropogenic climate change is a better phrase to use than simple climate change on its own. ☐ Climate change is a tautology that is like saying that water is wet! Of course water is wet and of course the climate and weather always keep changing! Since there is said to be no smoke without fire many voters and members of the public became increasingly alarmed about this new threat to our existence! Coal power stations would have to go and a whole new field of energy saving ideas would take their place.

Innovative ideas about saving energy soon began to flourish. An abundance of new age low grid technology started to blossom in the wake of the coal plant protests. There is no doubt that an exciting new era of green politics and energy innovation had arrived to the shores of Great Britain.

Suddenly the green pound was soaring and new companies were springing up to take advantage of a new market. Events at Oxford colleges promoted the new technologies and today there is a whole new field of expertise devoted to low carbon technology. This is all well and good.

Meanwhile Caroline Lucas had been elected as a Green MEP and had gone to Europe. While there she managed with fellow greens to instigate a new EU Directive called The Large Combustion Plant Directive. This EU Directive was issued in 2001 and the fate of our coal power stations was sealed. This Large Combustion Plant Directive would seriously impact on our energy security but no one batted an eye here in the United Kingdom.

You would think that any reasonably intelligent politician with his finger on the pulse would have seen a red flag waving. Playing with a nation`s power infrastructure is a very serious matter.

The amount of generating capacity of this closure of our power stations would be enormous.

Still one should never underestimate just how foolish a politician can be in the quest for votes and popularity! Unlike the Thatcher years, there was neither unrest nor miners` strikes to justify the plant closures.

We now face a serious energy deficit by the year 2025 when all of the power stations are decommissioned. There are multiple reasons for the predicted looming energy crisis.

At the moment we import coal at a very cheap price from America to run our coal power stations. America can sell coal cheaply to the U.K. as it has vast reserves of shale gas that it is now using. So at this point in time Great Britain is importing very cheap coal to run our fully operational coal power stations.

You would think that politicians would be thrilled at this serendipitous godsend of cheap imported coal from the USA. After all, cheap energy equals maximum profits and a buoyant economy. Well it seems that our inept policy makers do not appreciate a gift horse when it is staring them in the face. Instead of appreciating this economic gift of cheap imported coal the British Government has decided to embrace the most expensive energy policy possible. Welcome to blackout Britain!

Our once great Britain has come to a dark place where the demolition of our power stations will potentially bring us power blackouts. The Large Combustion Plant Directive will recklessly curtail our energy supply when the remaining power stations are blown up.

The intentions were good as it was genuinely believed by the politicians that the plants were emitting dangerous pollution. Soon there was an exponential growth in the idea that carbon is evil. I personally have no doubt that the politicians had good environmental intentions and may have genuinely believed that carbon dioxide was a perceived danger to mankind.

However the blaring fact of an imminent ice age had been completely overlooked in the rush to curb carbon emissions. In the excitement generated around in closing our coal power stations to avoid global warming, the overdue ice age had been ignored!

Donald Trump may have actually got it right with his desire to revive the coal industry. The new ice age will affect vast parts of America if previous glaciation records are correct! Therefore more energy will be needed to heat homes.

Blackout Britain may soon witness a return to the 1970`s winters of discontent. The saying that fools rush in where angels fear to tread could aptly apply to our reckless energy policy! When the ice age comes solar panels might freeze over and need constant clearing. Frozen wind turbine gears will start to malfunction.

There are many documented drawbacks of wind turbine energy production. **At wind speeds of 5 miles per hour, wind farms frequently consume more power than they**

produce. Wind energy accounts for only 4 % of total worldwide energy production and so it is obvious that we still need other forms of energy production to keep the lights on.

It has been reported by energy watchdogs that Britain will need 30 gas power plants by 2025 to plug the looming energy gap. However the warmists will not allow gas for heat either! They are proposing to ban all gas boilers in the future! The prospect of freezing winter fatalities has been glossed over to favour the global warming zeitgeist.

The Government is proposing to invest £200 billion of tax payers` money in energy generation which relies heavily on subsidies in order to remain viable. They are stubbornly choosing to turn their back on cheap coal imported from America.

The implications of tax payer subsidies for energy production are extremely serious. The cost of this decarbonising plan may rise to over £200 billion once new nuclear power is thrown in to the mix. This cost will then be passed on to the utility consumer.

A consumer with an increased electricity bill will have a proportionately lower disposable income as a result of paying a higher quarterly bill. This reduced spending power may further exacerbate the recessed economy in a negative feedback loop. The economy will spiral further into recession as consumers are restricted in their spending as a result of paying wind farm subsidies.

If the economy is in a deep depression then clearly the paying of subsidies via an increase in energy bill tariff will have a serious impact on consumers.

The British government will spend £110 billion in decarbonising the energy supply by the year 2020! This is fancy speak for shutting down our 15 viable coal power stations! So a lot of money is being thrown down the drain to prevent global warming when all of the geological records show that we are overdue an ice age!

If an ice age arrives we may be in serious trouble due to this decarbonisation strategy. Ice can build up on blades during a freezing cold winter anticyclone. This can cause gear box failure and blades can snap. If a heavy turbine blade ruptured near a residence it could be very dangerous.

There are other drawbacks of wind power such as the cube law of energy generation. For example, when the wind falls from 30 miles per hour to ten miles per hour the energy output falls by 96 per cent. Wind power is also intermittent and variable. If the weather is too windy turbines need to be shut down or they will break.

Turbines damage wildlife and the infrasound can be very unpleasant and may be linked to health problems. It has been reported that Infrasound vibrations of seven cycles per second cause anxiety and nausea.

Wind turbines do not always protect the environment and may damage the countryside, maiming birds and protected bats. Some rural campaigners think that the ugly pylons needed to convey electricity for wind turbines as well as the actual turbine itself are spoiling the beauty of the countryside. The gentrified landowners who are receiving large subsidies to have turbines on their land are mostly very appreciative of wind technology!

It is time for some innovative thinking for energy supply as I predict that one day all wind farms will be dismantled as they are really not that cost effective. If we really do have a mini ice age then investing in wind may prove a costly mistake.

The turbines we presently import from Denmark are very inefficient. The wind kite turbine can fly higher than a conventional wind turbine, reaching heights where wind tends to be stronger and more consistent. The saying "fools rush in…" springs to mind when we look at the huge amount of money our government has rushed to spend for an inefficient model of wind turbine. Furthermore the present day model of Danish imported wind turbine requires a lot of maintenance and our unwieldy turbines are prone to gearbox failure.

The consequences of such gear box failure may be demonstrated by the incident at Conisholme wind farm in January 2009. During a freezing cold spell of weather caused by an anticyclone blocking high weather system over Great Britain, the turbine blades snapped and fell to the ground. This turbine failure was caused by heavy ice build up and gear box failure on stationary blades as wind does not blow during freezing cold stationary blocking high weather systems.

UFO enthusiasts were keen to blame an alien encounter as being responsible for the damage and the snapped blades received widespread media coverage. During the freezing cold spell in January 2009 it was reported in the local press that an alien encounter occurred at Conisholme Wind Farm!

Witnesses reported seeing strange lights hovering above the wind farm. It seemed that a fleet of alien menacing UFOs were coming to invade our peaceful planet! The next day a broken turbine blade was found on the ground and another was bent at a strange angle. Did aliens come to inspect the innovative technology? A more prosaic explanation is that the freezing anti cyclone caused a gear box malfunction! The realistic explanation is that turbines are not a very suitable form of energy production in freezing weather conditions as the wind does not blow in a freezing anticyclone. Turbines do not function in freezing weather as ice builds up on the blades. Turbines need a lot of maintenance to keep them running smoothly and things can soon go wrong in sustained cold weather.

Wind will not blow in a cold winter anticyclone and blades become weighed down by ice. Turbines will therefore *not supply energy in a continuous cold weather spell.* In icy conditions a wind mast with a mass of 1000kg can accumulate 5000kg of ice! Turbine blades degrade quickly in icy weather as there is no torque or lift. Large accumulations of ice stop the anenometers from working altogether. It has also been stated in certain regions that wind turbines actually create a carbon monoxide problem in certain areas, which threatens the entire rationale of the supposedly low carbon wind farm industry!

During cold anticyclone weather systems known as blocking highs there is very little wind. These anticyclone cold high pressure systems are predicted to become more frequent in the coming low sunspot cycles, according to the work of Professor Mike Lockwood.

So just when we need electricity the most in our freezing winters the wind turbines will remain stationary for weeks on end! Unless turbine manufacturers can come up with an innovation so that turbines function in windless freezing conditions our country may suffer a serious energy deficit. Remember that in the cold future we will not be allowed gas boilers, nor coal and wood pellets may run out.

Great Britain is a very windy country so wind power should in theory be an asset. Our Government is very keen to expand wind power here in the British Isles. This is entirely understandable since we are a windswept country. However more work needs to be done to ensure that future turbines operate well under freezing anticyclone weather systems. The turbine design needs to be improved so as not to drain the national grid of energy when they are forced to shut down in high winds. More innovation is needed, but I am sure that our inventive country will eventually get to a solution!

In Mauna Loa, Hawaii, a wind farm lies abandoned due to the taxpayer subsidies running dry. There are many such abandoned wind farms worldwide. This should serve as a stark warning to taxpayers. Most of the U.K. energy policies are based on the premise of an imminent rise in temperatures due to a universal consensus that temperatures will rise. However, there is an equally compelling case for an imminent global cooling or a mini ice age.

We need to at least consider the impact that major cooling might have on our national energy security. If a mini ice age were to rapidly develop in the space of decades as may have happened in previous epochs, then our investment in wind technology may prove to have been a catastrophic mistake.

Our heating bills now contain a substantial surcharge to pay for measures to allegedly combat global warming. I hope the irony of this is not lost on shivering consumers! When the ice age hits people may become frustrated at the Government`s hasty global warming energy policies.

It is a galling paradox that despite using less energy, hard-pressed consumers are now paying higher utility bills. Clearly in some ways this paying more for less must be a regressive policy! Investing in new nuclear power stations is projected to further exacerbate price rises. The huge nuclear investment start-up costs will be added to consumers' bills causing meteoric rises in the next decade. A lot of policy errors are contributing to high energy bills and really Government should get a grip on its energy policy.

I am not convinced that biomass has been such a great idea either. This is because using trees for power stations has caused catastrophic deforestation in many parts of the world. The editor of the Ecologist agreed with me that the trend for biomass is causing harm to the planet as trees have leaves that reduce pollution. People like the trendy sound of biomass but caution is needed. Coal is not a great fuel, but at least it has no green leaves.

In my opinion, it is better to use cheap coal than burning trees which our planet desperately needs. **Drax concedes that 'when biomass is burned, carbon dioxide is released into the atmosphere'. Its defence is that trees – unlike coal or gas – are renewable** because they can grow again, and that when they do, they will neutralise the carbon in the atmosphere by 'breathing' it in, or in technical parlance, 'sequestering' it.

Drax spokespersons claim that burning wood reduces greenhouse gas emissions compared with coal-fired generation by as much as 80 per cent! Drax now profits from the Government's green energy subsidies. Last year, these amounted to a staggering £62.5 million, paid by levies on consumers' bills!

This is set to triple as Drax increases its biomass capacity. During recent cold spells the U.K. has nearly run out of gas on several occasions. Once we had just three hours left of gas capacity. Yet gas is also on the hit list to be eliminated as a fuel source as it is also considered to be a greenhouse gas. The powers that be would like it if we did not use gas at all. So forget your nice cosy gas fired central heating as it is considered to be causing global warming rather than in house warming!

A ground source heat pump is preferred and yet the costs would be astronomical for home owners. Such a heat pump will cost around thirteen thousand pounds and entail indescribable disruption to householders during installation! A confused and misguided Government has decreed that customers will pay £105 per MW/hr for biomass electricity. This is an exorbitant amount to pay for the supposedly green energy.

Burning precious trees for biomass is costing even more than power from the "white elephant" nuclear plant at

Hinkley Point in Somerset. Hinkley has been dubbed the most expensive nuclear power in station in the world and will cost at least £100 billion to construct! Of course the British government does not mind as costs will be passed on to consumers!

The Department for Energy and Climate Change announced that burning wood is sustainable, or carbon neutral" since trees can grow back! A lot of nonsense is now being spouted in the name of saving carbon emissions. Common sense should tell us that cutting down acres of woodland for fuel cannot possibly be good for the environment. If an ice age arrives, ships will not be able to import the felled logs for biomass. There may not be sufficient trees to burn if the ice buries them.

Meanwhile, Paris climate deals will allow the proliferation of costly but supposedly "low carbon" nuclear power stations. Whoever would have dreamt that nuclear power would now be labelled as green energy? It is foolish for this government to waste £24bn on constructing new nuclear plants such as Hinckley that will cause a meteoric rise in energy bills to pay for its construction, when we have one thousand years worth of free coal here. We can also import coal very cheaply from America at a fraction of the price to build new nuclear power stations such as Hinkley.

Acres of forest worldwide will be cut down to provide fuel for our biomass power stations that have replaced the coal. The concept behind biomass has been long forgotten along the blind climate alley. Biomass refers to dead or fallen wood on the ground that may be burnt as a so-called carbon neutral fuel. Biomass should not include deliberately felling forests of trees as is now happening in the name of green energy.

We are pursuing a lot of unusual ideas to replace the power that will be lost when our coal power stations are shut down. This closure is being forced on the basis of a hypothetical rise in temperatures that looks increasingly unlikely to materialise.

One of the saddest "eco" ideas is to burn biofuel. The amount of food that is now being burned as biofuels could nourish 200 million people! This is frankly immoral. The closure of our coal fired power stations was a strategic public health error as their emissions were mostly steam and particulate free.

When our cheap cost effective imported coal is burnt in our advanced coal power stations, all of the dirty particulate pollutants are removed by scrubbers. Most of the vapour cloud seen from the power station chimneys is comprised of harmless steam! Coal is only harmful to health when burnt in open hearth fires. When coal is burnt in a fireplace the emissions then become harmful to health as the resultant dirty smoke is not filtered as it is in a power station when burnt.

 Therefore if we face a power shortage and people start to burn coal or wood in their hearths, we will witness a regressive step. We will in effect be going back a century to the times when city skies were filled with smoke and respiratory disease was rife. So much for our clean energy revolution! Our clean running coal power stations that are earmarked for closure remove all of the harmful particulates. Yes we do need to explore many alternative forms of renewable energy such as wind and solar to add variety to our energy mix. However if an ice age dawns our wind farms will be all but useless and solar panels may ice over.

Recently there have been many power cuts in Oxfordshire. It looks increasingly likely that these power cuts are a direct result of our flawed energy policy to close down fully operational power stations such as Didcot power station in Oxfordshire. We have lost a huge amount of generational capacity as a result of this decision.

We should ideally have 25 per cent spare capacity but we are now down to just four per cent which is not enough to cope with peak demand. It is not the case that Didcot Power Station was past its sell-by date, as is the case with our ageing nuclear reactors. Didcot had recently undergone expensive improvements to its chimney stacks to give clean air emissions.

The following extract was written by myself and published by the Oxford Mail and other newspapers shortly before the Didcot power station was blown up:

"Next year Didcot Power Station in Oxfordshire will close to comply with the European Large Combustion Plant Directive. This is a strategic error that will cause economic and energy insecurity. Oxfordshire will lose half of its power supply. This looming energy gap, due to decentralisation of energy production, could cripple industry in a disturbing echo of the 1979 'winter of discontent'.

Look around your home or business and estimate how many electrical appliances you will need to throw away in order to achieve a 50 per cent reduction in energy use. No more electric guitars, computer games, kitchen gadgets, electric blankets or fast internet; the list is simply endless. There is a predicted energy deficit of around 10-16 GW due to power station closures, which may lead to power cuts if 50 per cent household energy savings are not made. We are gaily walking headlong into disaster.

Investment in wind technology alone will cost the taxpayer £200bn in the near future. OFGEM also estimates that £200bn of investment is needed for new infrastructure in the National Grid to prevent power cuts in the UK. In total at least £400-500bn more investment is needed to keep the lights on! This is not including the gargantuan investment needed for new nuclear power.

This is a lot of money in times of austerity. The UK is investing the gargantuan sum of money in order to prevent a hypothesised rise in temperatures. We are committing ourselves to the most stringent of carbon emissions in the entire world due to our unique 2008 Climate Change Act which was enacted by Ed Miliband when he was Climate Secretary.

This money will also have to come from hard-working taxpayers.

Consumers will be paying more for their electricity tariffs yet receiving less energy for their money. Countries that do not need to comply with this European directive, such as China are increasingly prosperous while Europe is becoming bankrupt."

The Oxford Mail gave it the title "the Green movement is bankrupting Europe". I was not too sure about the title as I consider myself to be an environmentalist even though I do not subscribe to the zeitgeist of an anthropogenic carbon dioxide induced warming. My main concern is that we exposing ourselves to power cuts.

In early March 2018 there were several power cuts in Great Britain and North America as the cold "Beast from the East" and polar vortex caused power shortages as people struggled to heat their homes .

It was also announced that the country had nearly run out of gas and chaos ensued as the country went into a snow induced meltdown. This is a small taste of things to come as when the ice age bites we will be lacking power to keep the lights on.

Nefarious schemes are often found to be brewing in our energy markets. A high profile case of corporate crime involving energy supply was the Enron scandal that erupted in 2001. This scam involved power cut malpractice with utility companies. Enron was a hugely successful American company listed by Fortune Magazine. Enron employed a creative accountant, who used numerous tricks to hide Enron`s liabilities.

This seemingly robust company encouraged investors to buy shares in a company that was in fact hiding colossal debts. The dishonesty of Enron was not confined to its creative accounting techniques. Enron had given large donations to the political campaign of a Californian Senator, Phil Gramm, who was duly elected. In return he passed legislation in 2000 to deregulate electricity commodities. This was beneficial to Enron who owned many power utilities. Following the legislation California had 38 serious rolling blackout power cuts!

These power cuts were deliberately engineered by Enron to maximise profits. Any one power cut can seriously endanger life since power is essential for hospitals. This wholly unacceptable behaviour of corporations has been discussed by criminologist Stephen Box who asserts that one is seven times more likely to be killed by corporate negligence than a common street criminal (Box 1983).

This fraud involved Ponzi schemes which pay off investors using other investors' money.

The Enron scandal shows how fraudsters were prepared to put lives at risk for their own gain. There may be parallel analogies between the coal power station closures and the Enron power scam. Power cuts may arise here in Great Britain as a result of corporate malfeasance. Already there has been a tragic accident at Didcot power Station as a result of the EU Directive to dismantle perfectly adequate non polluting power stations.

A country's prosperity depends on a cheap energy supply. It has been proven by psychologists that large groups often make very bad decisions. This phenomenon can be labelled as group think or a risky shift in behaviour.

For example the fatal decision to launch the Space Shuttle Challenger in freezing temperatures took place despite warnings from engineers about possible mechanical O ring failure in cold weather. The group decided to ignore the lone engineer's advice to abort the launch on a freezing January morning, with tragic consequences.

Psychologists have proven that a group of individuals often make riskier and unwise decisions as they feel that the sense of responsibility is shared and somehow diluted among the group. This social and psychological truism is known as the "risky shift" and may also apply to the reckless EU directives to close power stations. This closure in the face of predicted cold weather or worse is a very high risk strategy!

Psychological factors also affect the desire to conform. There have been many social psychology experiments that demonstrate that individuals prefer to conform to the group rather than stand out on a limb. This was fist demonstrated in the 1950`s by the work of Solomon Asch.

If we choose more expensive energy options such as Hinkley nuclear power plant this cost will be passed on to customers via their electricity bills. Hinkley Point has been dubbed the most expensive and least economic power station in the world.

Still at least we can say that it is a low carbon energy source even if it is high in plutonium! It seems that carbon has become more feared than radioactive isotopes! Yet we are a carbon based life form and indeed all life on Earth is carbon based.

Humans eat carbohydrates every day and carbon is ubiquitous on our carbon based planet. Therefore the idea that we can somehow curb carbon emissions seems somewhat impossible!

However even an astronomically expensive nuclear power station is far better than being without any power at all! When the ice age bites we will need all the power we can muster. Solar panels will not be able to generate as much power if snow and ice accumulates on them. Solar panel cells are wired together so that if one small part of a panel is snow covered it may shut down the whole system. People will have to start climbing onto their roofs to keep the solar panels clear if we experience heavier snowfalls. Welcome to ice age Britain!

Our energy policy has been skewed in the belief that our energy use will somehow affect the climate. This is not the case, yet whole swathes of the population have been brainwashed into believing that when they leave a light on it is warming the planet! Yes it is good to save energy and this is why the Government propaganda has been disseminated. The more energy we save, the better the grid will cope with coming power shortages.

However if an ice age bites we may be forced to use a lot more energy. Sadly if the microgeneration of energy continues along the trajectory of open fires and woodburners, clouds of brown hazy smoke will pollute our skies and deflect the incoming sunlight. The Clean Air Act of 1952 now seems to be all but redundant.

This pollution from burning wood will facilitate an anthropogenic cooling rather than a warming. Our present policy will most likely encourage this to happen. As temperatures cool in the coming decades, the United Kingdom will become colder and smokier unless we act now.

We need to keep our remaining non polluting coal power stations open. We should ignore the EU Large Combustion Plant Directive which played into the hands of the carbon traders under the guise of being a measure to protect the climate.

It is a paradox that despite using less energy hard-pressed consumers are now paying higher utility bills in Great Britain. Clearly in some ways this paying more for less *must* be a regressive policy. Yet somehow the exploited consumer has been persuaded to go along with paying this "green tariff" on their utility bills to allegedly cut carbon emissions.

It seems that cutting carbon emissions has become a euphemism for saving energy. At this point it gets confusing. We should most definitely be cutting down on pollution and emitting dirty aerosols and we should be endorsing electric cars and zero particulate emissions vehicles.

However we should *not* be closing down our non-polluting power stations and endangering countless lives through power cuts. Would you like to be in a hospital during a power cut? How will our manufacturing industry function with brownouts and reduced working hours?

If the solar cycles do indeed herald the dawn of a new ice age, the United Kingdom is going to be in a dire predicament as consumers will need more energy to keep warm. Instead of closing down or blowing up perfectly functioning power stations we should be looking to increase and preserve our energy infrastructure.

Nuclear fusion would be ideal if only it could be achieved. Sadly the idea of thermonuclear fusion and the work done in Culham has achieved little success to date. Investing in new nuclear power stations is projected to further exacerbate price rises. The huge nuclear investment start-up costs will be added to consumers' bills causing meteoric rises in the next decade.

A lot of policy errors are contributing to high energy bills and really Government should get a grip on its energy policy. Consumers are being encouraged to curtail energy use. This is undoubtedly a good idea because if we do not save energy we will face crippling power cuts when all of our remaining coal power stations are closed.

Therefore we are now being persuaded to accept a smart meter in our homes in order to monitor energy use. In theory it sounds like a good idea but there is always a hidden catch where utility companies are concerned.

The idea behind smart meters is for consumers to monitor their energy use

and hopefully cut down. However although I am keen on energy saving I have decided not to have a smart meter installed despite the advertising promising free electricity on weekends. The reasons the public is becoming wary of smart meters are as follows. Once a smart meter is installed the utility provider has complete control over the readings as well as the power supply.

There have been reported cases where homeowners received astronomically high bills that were incorrect that may be due to a software malfunction. The batteries are prone to suddenly dying thus potentially leaving a home without any electricity. There have been all kinds of software malfunction and it has been shown that these meters can be easily hacked into.

This could put us at the mercy of terrorists and cyber criminals. Hackers could cut the nation's power and hold it to ransom. A single line of malicious code could cut the power to a home or business. Hacking the meter could even lead to house fires as meters are primed to explode with simple instructions.

A hacker would have control over all of your smart devices in the home. A burglar would not even need to break in if he had control over the smart devices protecting your home. The smart meter could be used as a Trojan horse to gain access to computers and gadgets around the home.

All meters from one utility company use the same hardcode credentials so that a hacker can gain easily control of an entire network. This is because the network is not segmented so the whole lot is linked.

Smart meters also use very weak encryption so that it is child`s play for hackers. There are now 100 million smart meters worldwide partly thanks to Al Gore who promoted them for his business. In 2009 smart meters were hacked into en masse in Puerto Rico leading to a huge billing fraud. The cyber criminals inflated the bills then skimmed off the excess. This has been happening all over the world.

The universal rollout of these meters is a very bad idea for our national security and is yet another example of the follies of government policy. A rogue state such as North Korea could carry out a cyber attack that would over load the national grid leading to blackouts. Millions of homes could be plunged into darkness. The American Government announced that it feared a cyber attack on its national grid.

The spy centre, GCHQ in Cheltenham, is not pleased with the insecurity of smart meters and yet our inept policy makers want every home to have one! There were even reports in 2018 that Russia may try to hack into America`s power grid. The EU wants most homes to have smart meters.

The European Union is also behind the reckless EU Large Combustion Plant Directive which aims to blow up our functioning power stations! All of this folly has been enacted in the name of a global warming that is most unlikely to occur, and leaves us even less prepares for an ice age.

In 2018 the utility company SSE had to reassure its worried customers after a software upgrade resulted in bills that were thousands of pounds higher. It was reported that smart meters have been routinely charging consumers seven times the rate for electricity! Smart meters are easily confused by appliances such as low energy light bulbs or dimmer switches. Even a microwave oven can throw a smart meter off its tracks.

   It seems that smart meters benefit the supplier at the expense of the consumer. They also benefit a Government that wants us to use a lot less energy to cope with their reckless decision to blow up our power stations. Smart meters are also easily hacked into and this has already happened. The customer has no way of checking if a reading is correct as it is all done remotely via computer.

The boss of energy firm EDF admitted that customers are being given out of date smart meters as part of a Government campaign to roll out smart meters in 26 million British households. You have been warned! These inferior smart meters also make it impossible for a customer to switch to a cheaper energy supplier. Customers are being bullied into having a smart meter. However they are fully within their legal rights to refuse to have one installed.

There is even a plan afoot whereby smart meter customers will have their energy supply unexpectedly curtailed and lights dimmed as in brownouts, during peak times and winter to avoid power cuts. ☐ This is fine if you fancy having your lights dimmed for a quiet romantic evening, but it might spoil the rise your baked soufflé if the power suddenly turns down! In a nutshell be smart and do not accept a not so very smart meter!

Unfortunately these energy saving measures are now becoming almost mandatory as we face a looming energy gap due to our premature closure of our fully functioning non polluting power stations. This coal power station closure was encouraged by carbon entrepreneurs who would make a profit from complex carbon trading schemes. Great Britain is now facing a loss of power in the coming decades unless this EU Large Combustion Plant Directive is reversed. This policy reversal should take place as a matter of national security in order to protect our power supply.

The pursuit of so called green energy schemes is proving very costly to the consumer. The cost of investing in innovative energy infrastructure is being gaily passed on to the consumer by our Government. The politicians seem not to have a care in the world for those who exist on lower incomes than themselves. Each and every customer will now pay a larger amount for their electricity in order to fund the new low carbon schemes. So while the carbon entrepreneurs become richer the exploited bill payer becomes ever poorer.

The Audit Committee estimates around £200 a year is being added on to consumers bills each year. Literally £billions of tax payers money is being spent on new ideas such as biomass boilers. Billions of pounds of public money is to be spent on 'green' boilers, despite evidence from the government's own experts and industry that they will do little to help the UK meet its energy targets.

A report from Brussels said that the Department of Energy and Climate Change (DECC) found that biomass boilers in the non-domestic sector were around 10-20% less efficient than expected. Those boilers account for 90% of payments under the Renewable Heat Incentive (RHI). The RHI is the government's flagship scheme to encourage a shift to low carbon heating (Neslen 2015).

The Government has pushed biomass boilers as a technology to help meet EU targets of getting at least 15% of its energy from renewable sources by 2020. The hope is that businesses and individuals will switch to wood burners or biomass boilers in return for payments under the RHI. However under-performance appears widespread in the UK biomass heat sector .

The final cost in public money could be over £10bn because the recipients installing biomass boilers receive annual payments from Renewable Heating Incentive for several years.

The Department for Energy and Climate`s own impact assessment shows that the wood pellet boilers are not cost nor energy efficient. In other words a lot of heat is being wasted as precious trees are going up in smoke; and all in the name of being a green policy! Our cheap to run coal power stations will be blown up or converted to burn wood pellets .

The irony is that burning wood pellets for energy is probably one of the most environmentally damaging ways of producing energy! So far, most Renewable Heat Incentive payments appear to have been banked by wealthy landowners and the long suffering taxpayer is funding this needless to say!

It seems that the Holy Grail quest for "low carbon" energy is coming in at quite a cost to the public purse. Billions of pounds are syphoned off and this money is accumulating into the hands of already wealthy individuals and corporations.

The ECO green schemes to insulate homes are obviously very useful indeed.

The Government blithely announced in 2018 that it was banning all gas for heating and cooking by the year 2050! The new "clean growth strategy" to save the planet from frying will wage a war on gas. So no more frying with gas in the future! Energy Ministers have vowed to phase out the use of gas by the year 2050!

Readers might recall that 2050 is possibly the year of the ice age. This ban on gas is all part of the legally binding laws we have passed to cut green house emissions by 2050.

From the year 2025 all new build rural homes will have ground source heat pumps instead of gas boilers. The Energy Secretary said that banning gas would ensure we are world leaders in cutting emissions!

All gas power plants must close by the 2030`s which is just when our Sun powers down. The Grantham Research Unit of Climate Change warned that Britain`s cosy days of cooking with gas are numbered! Soon our gas ovens will be relegated to the archives of oblivion and we will pay thorough the nose for more expensive electricity cookers!

In 2013 the United Kingdom almost ran out of gas in winter due to a dispute between Russia and the Ukraine. The reserves went down to a mere six hours worth of gas.

The Russian company Gazprom sells around 16 million cubic meters of gas to Great Britain every year.

This imported gas comes via Europe and Norway. Up to 40 per cent of the European gas is imported from Russia. Therefore we need to keep relations on an amicable note with Russia lest a new cold war results in cold homes!

The gas supply nearly ran out again in March 2018 and a mere three hours supply was left. Britain had to buy a shipment of liquefied gas from Russia to cope with the demand. This time the gas shortage was blamed on the decision to close a gas storage facility off the coast of Yorkshire called the Rough storage facility.

This closure means that we lose up to 70 per cent of our gas storage. If the weather gets colder in the future we will simply run out of gas. Indeed it was reported in March 2018 many rural British homeowners did run out of liquefied gas and had no heat for days.

Some Government ministers are concerned about this dependency on

Russian gas imports. Perhaps this reliance on unreliable foreign gas imports might explain the recent interest in British shale gas deposits. However fracking for shale is a very unpopular idea due to fears of contamination of the water table with fracking chemicals.

There are also concerns of instability and earth tremors. Due to the environmental problems it is unlikely that fracking for shale gas will be given the green light. It has been said that there may only be around five years worthy of shale gas in Great Britain anyway which makes it hardly seem worth the costs to the landscape.

The plan to phase out gas completely originated at the Paris Climate Deal. So once your gas boiler breaks down you will have to replace it with more costly electric heating. Impoverished broken gas boiler owners may face being cold and unable to cook proper meals if they cannot afford an expensive electric or heat pump replacement.

Unless you are comfortably well off you will suffer because of the Paris climate deals. Pensioners will succumb to hypothermia and many will simply go without heat once gas is banned.

I am not sure how the North Sea oil industry fits into the low carbon climate legislation. There do not appear to be any plans to stop drilling for oil off the shores of Scotland. I find it strange that somehow this industry has escaped the protests from environmentalists. Perhaps it is impossible to get out to the rigs!

Scotland`s First Minister would not appreciate any interference in their precious oil reserves!

   The revenues from the oil are projected at £57 bn for 2018. This is vital revenue for the Scottish Government. North Sea oil has become a key campaign issue in Scotland, so unsurprisingly one does not hear of many protests against it! It was reported in the Guardian newspaper that the oil giant Shell plans to drill for new oil fields in 2018. This is probably a good idea with an ice age coming.

   Really our Government needs to get a sensible grip on energy policies. Frankly our energy policy is something of a basket case! We have pursued the most expensive ways to generate electricity and put ourselves at risk of future power cuts. All of this has been done to avert a hypothetical rise in temperatures! **While all of these shenanigans are taking place in energy markets, there is the looming possibility of a mini ice age arriving!**

If the predictions of solar physicists are correct we will need to increase our energy production to cope with future icy cold winters. If a new mini ice age arrives and we have closed our 15 coal power stations and banned gas what will happen?

Unimaginable chaos may result as power cuts ensue and pensioners start dropping like flies in the cold. How ironic it will be if the Northern Hemisphere descends into an ice age and we do not have sufficient energy to keep warm because we closed our power stations to prevent global warming!

Conclusion:
Forewarned is Forearmed.

The more technologically advanced a civilisation, the greater a potential descent into anarchy. Any society using technology that depends on binary code is at risk of collapse into complete anarchy. If a major ice age arrives, then those who live a basic self- sufficient lifestyle will be in the best position to survive. If an ice age arrives suddenly, then those who live with their own power supply and source of food will also fare better. If a major ice age arrives, then those who live a basic self sufficient lifestyle will be in the best position to survive.

Great Britain is in a very precarious position as we are so near to the Arctic Circle. It seems that all of our Northern Hemisphere climatic feedback loops are conspiring towards an ice age for Great Britain! There is very little likelihood therefore of a warm balmy Mediterranean climate returning to Great Britain. This is a prediction that climate modellers have got completely wrong. The climate feedback loops will always result in Great Britain *becoming cooler rather than warmer.* This is why the title of my book is "Ice Age Britain".

The general public has been led to believe that the main drivers of our climate are the greenhouse gases. In fact the main climatic drivers are as follows: solar activity, the Coriolis force, jet streams, the hydrosphere, wind patterns, ocean circulation patterns, Milankovitch orbital variables, cosmic dust, sulphur aerosols, volcanic eruptions, cosmic rays and cloud cover, to name a few! Phew!

On a serious note, I wrote this book not because I hanker for fame but as a matter of national security. We must start to prepare for the ice age that will inevitably arrive on our shores. In the United States there are up to three million survivalists who are prepared for a collapse of our modern day society. When the national grid collapses, they will burn the wood from their land to cook and keep warm. When the infrastructure to deliver food breaks down, the prepared survivalists will have home grown food and will hunt for wild animals.

The Earth has been steadily cooling down over the last 60 million years and the last two million years have been the coldest ever recorded! Since Earth is on a multi-million year downward cooling trend, we may get the mother of all ice ages. The next ice age may be even deadlier than the last ice age when the world population shrunk to only a few million. We will soon be reaching the end of the safe Holocene. Once more we will plunge into an ice age so severe that it may even spell the end of humanity. You have been warned!

References

Abe-Ouchi A., Saito, F., Kawamura K., Raymo M., Okuno J., Takahashi K., Blatter H., Insolation-driven 100,000-year glacial cycles and hysteresis of ice-sheet volume *Nature* 500 p 150-193 8 August 2013

Ackerman, A. S., et al. (2000). "Effects of Aerosols on Cloud Albedo: Evaluation of Twomey's Parameters of Cloud Susceptibility Using Measurements of Ship Tracks." *Journal Atmospheric Sciences* **57**: 2684-95.

Alvarez et al, (1980), "Extraterrestrial cause for the Cretaceous –Tertiary extinction", *Science,* 208 (4448):1095-1108)

Asch, S.E. (1951). "Effects of group pressure on the modification and distortion of judgments" in H. Guetzkow (Ed.) *Groups, leadership and men* (pp.177–190) Pittsburgh, PA: Carnegie Press.

Alvarez, W. et al (1980)"Extraterrestrial cause for the Cretacious-Tertiary Extinction" *Science* vol. 208 pp 1095-1108.

Anklin, M. et al "Climate instability during the last interglacial period recoded in the GRIP ice core *Nature* vol 364 pp203-207 15 July 1993(GRIP) 1993

Arrhenius, Svante "On the Influence of Carbonic Acid in the Air upon the Temperature of the Ground*" Philosophical Magazine and Journal of Science* Series 5, Volume 41, April 1896, pages 237-276.

Behringer, W. (1999): Climatic Change and Witch-hunting: the Impact of the Little Ice Age on Mentalities. *Climatic Change*, Vol.1(1): 335-351

Bell, A. and Strieber, W. (2000).*The coming global superstorm*, Pocket Books, New York,

Betts, A. K. and Ball, J. H., "Albedo over the boreal forest".*J. Geophys. Res.* **102, D24**, 28901–28909 (1997)

Biello, D. "Did a Comet hit Earth 12000 Years Ago". *Scientific American* Jan 2 2009.

Biello, D. (July 18, 2012). "Controversial Spewed Iron Experiment Succeeds as Carbon Sink". *Scientific American* July 19, 2012).

Bond, G., et al (2001) "Persistent solar influence on North Atlantic climate during the Holocene". *Science* 294: 2130-2136

Bowen, D.Q., (1978) *Quaternary geology: A stratigraphic framework for multidisciplinary work*, Pergamon Press Oxford, New York,

Box, S. (1983) *Power, Crime and Mystification*, London: Tavistock.

Broecker, W.S. "Unpleasant surprises in the greenhouse?" *Nature*, vol. 328, pp. 123-126, 1987

Bryden, H. L. et al "Atlantic currents show sign of weakening" *Nature* **438**, 655-657 (December 1 2005) .

Calder, N. "The Arithmetic of Ice Ages", *Nature,* Vol. 252, pp. 216-18, 1974

Calder, N. 1999 scientific paper: *'The Carbon Dioxide Thermometer', Energy & Environment,* 1999, Vol. 10, pp. 1-18

Cardiff University (2016, October 26). "Why does our planet experience an ice age every 100,000 years?" *Science Daily* Retrieved February 22, 2017

Carlson, A. E. (2013) "The Younger Dryas Climate Event" *Encyclopedia of Quaternary Science* **3** Elsevier pp.126–34.

Carrington,D. "Britain`s damp, leaky homes among most costly to heat" *The Guardian Newspaper* 29 November 2013

Casey, J.L. "Cold Sun" (2011) Trafford publishing

Castro, J. "Mountains may suck up carbon better than thought", Jan 16 20 *Live Science Online*

Champion, D. E., Lanphere, M. A., and Kuntz, M. A., 1988, "Evidence for a new geomagnetic reversal from Lava flows in Idaho: Discussion of short polarity reversals in the Brunhes and late Matuyama polarity chrons," *Journal of Geophysics Res.*, Vol. 93, p. 11667-11680, 10 Oct. 1988

Charlesworth, J. K. (1957) *The Quaternary era*, Edward Arnold, London

Clark, W. 1974, "Energy for Survival, the Alternative to Extinction", Better World Books

CLIMAP (1981) "Seasonal reconstructions of the Earth's surface at the last glacial maximum" in *Map Series*, Technical Report MC-36. Boulder, Colorado: Geological Society of America.

Cohen, J., et al "Recent Arctic amplification and extreme mid-latitude weather" *Nature geoscience* 7, 2014 pp 627-637

Crowther,T.W., Stephen M Thomas, Daniel S Maynard, Petr Baldrian, Kristofer Covey, Serita D Frey, Linda TA van Diepen, Mark A Bradford "Biotic interactions mediate soil microbial feedbacks to climate change" (2015/6/2) Proceedings of the National Academy of Sciences PNAS vol 112, issue 22 pp 7033-7038

Dansgaard, W. et al. (1993) "Evidence for general instability of past climate from a 250-kyr ice-core record". *Nature* **364** (6434): 218–220

Davies, R. (Oct 7 2016) *the Guardian* "Kite power to take flight in Scotland next year"

Day, S. J; Carracedo, J. C; Guillou, H. & Gravestock, P. (1999) "Recent structural evolution of the Cumbre Vieja volcano, La Palma, Canary Islands: volcanic rift zone re-configuration as a precursor to flank instability"*J. Volcanol. Geotherm Res.* 94, 135–167.

Dowdeswell and White, "Greenland ice Core Records and Rapid Climate Change" *Philosophical Transactions: Physical Sciences and Engineering* Vol. 352, No. 1699, *The Arctic and Environmental Change (*Aug. 15, 1995), pp. 359-371

Dowdy, Andrew; et al (2007) "Polar mesosphere and lower thermosphere dynamics: Response to sudden stratospheric warmings". *J. Geophys. Res*. **112**:

Elliot, M., Labeyrie, L., and Duplessy, J.C. 2002 "Changes in North Atlantic deep-water formation associated with the Dansgaard-Oeschger temperature oscillations (60-10 ka)". Quaternary Science Reviews 21: 1153-1165.

Evan, A. T., and Norris, J. R., (2012): On global changes in effective cloud height. Geophys. Res. December 2003 "Observed global cloud and radiation flux changes since 1952", American Geophysical Union

Eddy, J. A. (June 1976) "The Maunder Minimum*" Science* 192.

Kelso, J. and Danneman, M., 2017 "The contribution of Neanderthals to phenotypic variation on modern humans" *American Journal of Human Genetics* vol, 101: pp, 1-12

Kerry E.; et al (July 20, 1995) "Hypercanes: A Possible Link to Global Extinction Scenarios". *Journal of Geophysical Research* **100** (D7): 13755–13765.

Erickson, J. (2001) "Lost Creatures of the Earth: Mass Extinction in the History of life" Facts on File publishing books, New York

Europa (April 6 2006) "EU climate change policies: Commission asks member states to fulfil their obligations".

Felix R., (2000) "Not by Fire but by Ice" Sugarhouse Publishing

Fleming J.R. (2005) "Historical Perspectives on Climate Change". Oxford University Press pp. 69–70(Details of Tyndall's device for measuring the infrared absorptive power of a gas)

Fitzgerald, R.G. & Gleadow, A.J.W., 1988, Fission-track geochronology, tectonics and structure of the Transantarctic Mountains in northern Victoria Land, Antarctica. *Chemical Geology* (Isotope Geoscience Sections), **73**, 169-98

Francis, J.A., Vavrus, S.J. "Evidence for a wavier jet stream in response to rapid Arctic warming." 2015 *Environment Research Lett.* 10 014005

Francis, J. and Skific, N. "Evidence linking rapid Arctic warming to mid-latitude weather pattern *Philo Trans A Math Phys Eng Sci.* 2015 Jul 13; 373(2045): 20140170.

Frolich C., "Solar Irradiance Variability since 1978. Revision of the PMOD Composite during Solar Cycle 21"*Space Science Reviews,* Volume 125, Issue 1-4, pp. 53-65, August 2006

Ganopolski A. et al; *Nature* **529**, 200–203 (14 January 2016)

Glatzmaier, G.A. and Roberts P. H 1995 "a three dimensional self consistent model of a geomagnetic field reversal" *Nature.* 377 pp 203-209

Gosden, E. Jan 16 2015 "Labour energy price freeze 'preventing £130 bill cuts; Consumers are stuck paying high gas and electricity prices as a result of Ed Miliband's policy, " *the Telegraph*

Greenpeace Press Release March 4, 2016 "Fukushima nuclear disaster will impact forests, rivers and estuaries for hundreds of years".

Gribbin, J. (1990)"Hothouse Earth; the Greenhouse effect and Gaia" Bantam press

Gribbin, J. (1988)"The Hole in the Sky; Man`s Threat to the Ozone Layer", a Corgi book by Transworld Publishers Ltd

Hand,E. "Crippled Atlantic currents triggered ice age climate change" *Science* June 30 2016

Hansen,J. (2010) "Storms of my grandchildren" publisher Bloomsbury, N.Y.

Haug, G.H., "How the Isthmus of Panama put ice in the Arctic" *Oceanus Magazine* 22 March 2004, 2017

Hays J.D. (1976) "Variations in the earth's orbit: Pacemaker of the ice ages," Science, vol. 194, pp. 1121–1132.

Hays, J.D. Imbrie, J.; Shackleton, N.J. (1976) *"Variations in the Earth's Orbit: Pacemaker of the Ice Ages". Science* **194** *(4270): 1121–1132.*

Henry L. G., McManus J. F., Curry W. B., Roberts N. L., Piotrowski A. M., Keigwin L. D., North Atlantic Ocean circulation and abrupt climate change during the last glaciation, *Science* 29 July 2016: Vol. 353, Issue 6298, pp. 470-474

Higgins et al, "Sediment focusing creates 100-ka cycles in interplanetary dust accumulation on the Ontong Java Plateau," *Earth and Planetary Science Letters* 203 (2002) 383-397

Hoyle, F. "ice the ultimate human catastrophe* Amazon 1979, 1983

Howard, B. C., "Bizarre earthquake lights finally explained"   *National Geographic* Jan 7 2014

Imbrie, John and Imbrie, Katherine Palmer, (1979) Ice Ages: Solving the Mystery Enslow Publishers, Short Hills, NJ

Imbrie,J.et al. "On the structure and origin of major glaciation cycles, linear responses to Milankovich forcing" *Paleoceanography* **7**, 701–738 (1992).

Jackson, L. C., Peterson, K. A., Roberts, C. D. and Wood, R. A.; "Recent slowing of Atlantic overturning circulation as a recovery from earlier strengthening"; *Nature Geoscience* (2016).

Jaworowski, Z., 1994, *Ancient atmosphere - validity of ice records*, Environmental Science and Pollution Research, **1**(3): p. 161-171.

Jaworowski, Z., T.V. Segalstad, and N. Ono, (1992) *"Do* glaciers tell a true atmospheric CO_2 story" *The Science of the Total Environment*, **114**, p. 227-284.

Kennet, J.P. and Watkins, N. D., "Geomagnetic polarity change, volcanic maxima and faunal extinction in the south Pacific" *Nature*, Vol 227, p 930 -9934 , August 29 1970.

Kenyon, Scott J., Benjamin C. Bromley (2004) *"Stellar encounters as the origin of distant Solar System objects in highly eccentric orbits" Nature* **432** (7017): 598–602.

Khaitovitch et al (*Nature* online communications, April 2014).

Kerry et al "Hypercanes: a possible link in global extinction scenarios, *Journal of Geophysical Research*, vol.100,pp 13755-13765, July 20 1995

Kirby K. J. et al (2016). "Long-term changes in the tree and shrub layers of a British nature reserve and their relevance for woodland conservation management" *Journal for Nature Conservation*, 31, 51-60

Komitov, B., and Kaftan Vladimir "The sunspot cycle no. 24 in relation to long term solar activity" *Journal of Advanced Research* March 30 2013

Kopp, R.E. "The Paleoproterozoic snowball Earth: A climate disaster triggered by the evolution of oxygenic photosynthesis", Division of Geological and Planetary Sciences, California Institute of Technology 170-25, Pasadena, CA 91125; Communicated by Paul F. Hoffman, Harvard University, Cambridge, MA, June 14, 2005

Kukla, G.J. Matthews, R. J. (1972) "When will the present interglacial end?" *Science* **178** (4057) 190-202

Kukla,George J., et al (1972) "The end of the present Interglacial." *Quaternary Research* **2**: 261-69.

Lamb, H. H. (1995) "Climate history and the Modern World" Routledge publishing

Lee, X. et al "Observed Increase in Local Cooling Effect of Deforestation at Higher Latitudes," *Nature* 17   nov. (2011). *Nature 479 pp 384-387*

Leyser T. B. and A. Y. Wong "Powerful electromagnetic waves for active environmental research in geospace" (*Reviews of Geophysics*, Vol. 47, RG1001, 2009).

Lovelock, J., Epton, S, "The Quest for Gaia", *New Scientist*, 65, 934:304. Feb 6 1975

MacDonald, Francis, *Calibrating the Cryogenian,* Science, 5 March 2010: Vol. 327 no. 5970 pp. 1241-1243 5 March 2010

Malley, C.S., Johan C.I. Kuylenstierna, Harry W. Vallack, Daven K. Henze, Hannah Blencowe, Mike R. Ashmore. "Preterm birth associated with maternal fine particulate matter exposure: A global, regional and national assessment". *Environment International*, Feb 10   2017

Mann, M.E. (April 1 2014) "Earth will cross the climate danger threshold by 2036", *Scientific American.*

Markham,D. "5 hour energy creator to roll out pedal powered energy solution in India" *Treehugger blog* Oct 6 2015

Marvel, K., G.A. Schmidt, R.L. Miller, and L. Nazarenko, 2016: Implications for climate sensitivity from the response to individual forcings *Nature Climate Change*, **6**, no. 4, 386-389,

Mc Guire, B. (1999) Apocalypse, a History of Natural Disasters World books ltd.

Melamed M L; Michos E.D.; Post W.; Astor, B. (2008) "25-hydroxyl Vitamin D Levels and the Risk of Mortality in the General Population" *Arch. Intern. Med.* **168** (15): 1629–37.

Mesnage R., Renney G., Seralini G. E., Ward M., Antoniou M. "Multiomics reveal non-alcoholic fatty liver disease in rats following chronic exposure to an ultra-low dose of Roundup herbicide" *Scientific Reports* **7** Article number: 39328 (2017)

Miller, G.H., et al Abrupt onset of the Little Ice Age triggered by volcanism and sustained by sea-ice/ocean feedbacks. *Geophysical Research Letters*, 2012

Milne, A. "Earth's changing climate; the cosmic connection" Prism Press 1989

Moffa-Sánchez,P., Andreas Born, Ian R. Hall, David J. R. Thornalley, Stephen Barker "Solar forcing of North Atlantic surface temperature and salinity over the past millennium". *Nature Geoscience*, 2014

Moon, M. "Japan's most powerful X-Ray satellite is dead" April 29, 2016 *Space*

Nahle, N., 'Determination of Mean Free Path of Quantum/Waves and Total Emissivity of the Carbon Dioxide Considering the Molecular Cross Section' (2011), *Biology Cabinet*, (Peer Reviewed by the Faculty of Physics of the University of Nuevo Leon, Mexico).

NASA briefing "Sep 23 2008" Solar Wind loses power: Hits 50 year low".
NASA Facts Changing Global Cloudiness June 1999

Neslen, A. "Green biomass boilers may waste billions in public money". Jan 14 2015, *the Guardian Newspaper*
New Scientist, "Universe's highest electric current found" June 15 2011

Overland, J.E. Klaus Dethloff, Jennifer A. Francis, Richard J. Hall, Edward Hanna, Seong-Joong Kim, James A. Screen, Theodore G. Shepherd, Timo Vihma "Nonlinear response of mid-latitude weather to the changing Arctic". *Nature Climate Change*, 2016; 6 (11): 992

Overland J. and Wang, M."Large-scale atmospheric circulation changes associated with the recent loss of Arctic sea ice. *Tellus,* March 2009

Penn, M. and Livingston, W.,(2010) "long term evolution of sunspot magnetic fields" *IAU symposium* no 273

Petit J.R., Jouzel J., Raynaud D., Barkov N.I., Barnola J.M., et al. June 3 1999, Climate and Atmospheric History of the Past 420,000 years from the Vostok Ice Core, Antarctica, *Nature* 399: 429-436.

Petoukhov, V., Ramstorf, S., Petri, S., Shellnhumer, H.J., (Jan 16 2013), "Quasiresonant amplification of planetary waves and recent Northern Hemisphere weather extremes" PNAS.

Pierrehumbert R.T. (2010) "Principles of planetary Climate", Cambridge University Press.

Pierce, Jeffrey R.: Weisenstein, Debra K.: Heckendorn, Patricia: Peter, Thomas: Keith, David W., (Sep 2010) "Efficient formation of stratospheric aerosol for climate engineering by emission of condensable vapor from aircraft", *Geophysical Research Letters*, Volume 37, Issue 18, 18805.

Popova, E., Zharkova, V. and Zharkov, S "Probing latitudinal variations of the solar magnetic field in cycles 21–23 by Parker's Two-Layer Dynamo Model with meridional circulation "*Ann Geo*. Nov 20 2013

Preston.A., Dutton, W.R. and Harvey B.R., "Detection estimation, and radiological significance of silver 110m in oysters in the Irish Sea and the Blackwater Estuary" *Nature* pp 689-690

Rahmstorf,S. (2003) "The concept of the thermohaline circulation" *Nature* **421** (6924): 699.)

Rahmstorf,S. "Ice Cold in Paris" *New Scientist* Feb 8 1997 p, 26

Rees, J. "Green taxes stoke up steel plant jobs crisis',Northern Powerhouse is dealt a blow as Ministers are blamed for 3,000 redundancies" *Financial Mail on Sunday* Sep 19 2015

G.C.Reid, J.R.Mcafee,P.J.Crutzen, "Effects of intense ionisation events" *Nature* pp 489-492 October 12 1978

Roderick,M. I., Farquhar,G. D., (The Cause of Decreased Pan Evaporation over the Past 50 Years *Science* 15 Nov. 2002: Vol. 298, Issue 5597, pp. 1410-1411

Royal Astronomical Society "Irregular heartbeat of the Sun driven by double dynamo" July 9 2015.

Sagan, C. and Mullen, G., "Earth and Mars, Evolution of Atmospheres and Surface temperatures" *Science* July 7 1972

Sankararamen, S. et al, "The genomic landscape of Neanderthal ancestry in modern day humans" *Nature* vol; 507 p 354-356, 20 March 2014

Schnepp, E. and Hradetzky, H., 1994, "Combined paleointensity and 40Ar/39Ar age spectrum data from volcanic rocks of the West Eifel (Germany): Evidence for an early Brunhes geomagnetic excursion," *Journal of Geophysics Res.*, Vol. 99, p. 9061-9076, 10 May 1994.

Science Daily (2010) Link between solar activity and the UK's cold winters April 19, 2010 S*ource: Institute of physics*

Samsel, A, and Seneff, S. "Glyphosate, pathways to modern diseases II: Celiac sprue and gluten intolerance" *Interdisciplinary Toxicology* 2013 Dec; 6(4): 159–184.

Service R.F., *Science online* Jan. 11, 2017 "Here's how to improve controversial carbon accounting tool says U.S. science academy"

Science Daily "Ozone at lower latitudes is not recovering, despite Antarctic ozone hole healing." 6 February 2018.

Seager, R., D. S. Battisti, J. Yin, N. Gordon, N. H. Naik, A. C. Clement and M. A. Cane, (2002): "Is the Gulf Stream responsible for Europe's mild winters?" *Quarterly Journal of the Royal Meteorological Society,* 128(586): 2563-2586.

Shaviv and Veiser (2003) "Celestial driver of Phanerozoic Climate" *GSA Today* Vol. 13 no 7 July 2013

Speight, M. R. Henderson, P.A. "Marine Ecology: Concepts and Applications", Wiley- Blackwell 2010.

J.A. Screen, and I. Simmonds, "Amplified mid-latitude planetary waves favour particular regional weather extremes", *Nature Climate Change,* vol. 4, pp. 704-709, 2014.

Smith, C.R. The Native People of North America *Arctic Culture Area*

9 March 2000

Stanhill, G.; Moreshet,S. (2004-11-06). "Global radiation climate changes in Israel". *Climatic Change* 22(2): 121-138

Svensmark, H. and Calder, N. (2007) *The chilling stars, a new theory of climate change,* Amazon

Thompson, S.L.: Schneider Stephen H.: Neon Winter, Summer 1986, *Foreign Affairs*, Vol.64, No. 5, pp 981-1005

Tickell, O. (2008)." Kyoto 2: How to Manage the Global Greenhouse".(Zed Books Ltd)

Travis, David J., Carleton, Andrew M. & Lauritsen, Ryan G (2002). "Contrails reduce daily temperature range" *Nature*. **418** (6898): 601.)

Turco, **R.P., Toon O. B. , Ackerman T.P., Pollack J.B. , and Carl Sagan** "Global Atmospheric Consequences of Nuclear War" *Science* 222 pp 1283-1292 , 1983 .TTAPS

Vihma, T. "Effects of Arctic Sea Ice Decline on Weather and Climate": Finnish Meteorological Institute, *Surveys in Geophysics*, 30 January 2014.

Wigley, T.M.l., "A combined mitigation/geoengineering approach to climate stabilisation" *Science* Sep 14 2006

Wilson Clark, *Energy for Survival: The Alternative to Extinction (Garden City, NY: Anchor Books, 1974), p. 117).*

Woillard, G. M., 1979 "Abrupt end of the last interglacial in northeast France" *Nature* vol. 281 p 558-562 18 October 1979

Woods, T. "Press Release Shrinking atmosphere linked to low levels of solar radiation," LASP Lab. For Atmospheric and Space physics, Aug 26 2010

Wright, H. E. Jr., "Late Quaternary Vegetational History of North America," in Late Cenozoic Glacial Ages, Karl Turekian editor Yale publishing, p. 425-464, 1971

Willerslev et al Genomic structure in Europeans dating back at least 36,200 years *Science* Nov 6 2014

Yang Q., Dixon T. H., Meyers P. G., Bonin J., Chambers D., van den Broeke M. R., Ribergaard M. H., Mortensen "Recent increases in Arctic freshwater flux affects Labrador Sea convection and Atlantic overturning circulation" *Nature Communications* **7**, Article number: 10525 Jan 22 (2016)

Yin,S. "The Brilliance of a Stradivari Violin Might Rest Within Its Wood", *NY Times.* December 20, 2016.

Zharkova,V.V. *et al*. "Heartbeat of the Sun from Principal Component Analysis and prediction of solar activity on a millennium timescale", *Sci. Rep*. **5**, 15689; doi: 10.1038/srep15689 (2015).

Susan Thomas is a best-selling author who has written fifteen books, including scholarly books on the ice ages, maximum lifespan, Alzheimer`s Disease and a book called "Criminal Defenses" which is based on the biology of crime and bad behaviour.

She is an Oxford, United Kingdom resident and graduated in Psychology with Statistics and post graduated in Criminology and Criminal Justice.

She is active politically and is directly descended from the politician David Lloyd George on the Welsh side of her family.

She is also busy bringing up five children and hobbies include the I Ching and reading the runes.

Ice cover during the last ice Age

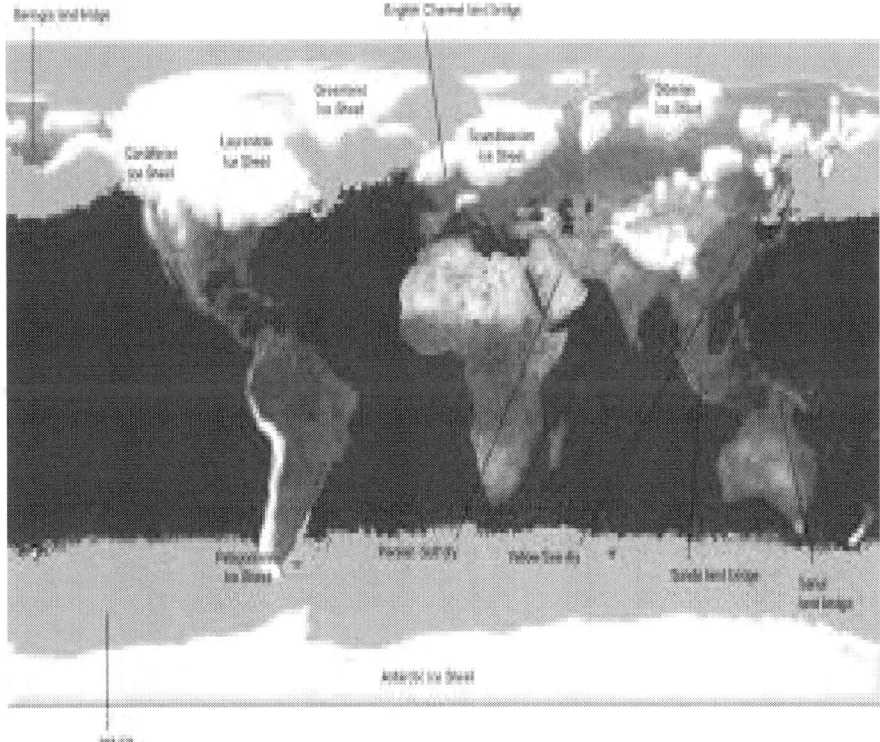

498

Printed in Great Britain
by Amazon